Praise for *The Other Half of Church*

This book is genius. It will soon be a standard among discipleship experts. If you have ever been frustrated at the hit-or-miss success of the church's ability to guide people into real life change, this book is for you. It not only explains why traditional discipleship has struggled; it offers practical advice for creating a truly transformational discipleship culture. Jim's expertise along with Michel's experience and easy reading style make this book a game changer in discipleship ministry.

MARCUS WARNER, President, Deeper Walk International

This masterfully crafted book about God's design for our brains and how it influences spiritual growth unmasks left-brain dominance in the church and skillfully shows that the right brain is the primary driver of character change and spiritual formation. Biblical teaching, measurable strategies, and practical exercises unfold how to nurture right-brain graces of covenant love, joy, gratitude, and group identity, resulting in the goals of personal and congregational transformation. In decades of ministry, I haven't engaged a book with such spiritual potential and power. Enthusiastically recommended.

BRUCE DEMAREST
Author and Senior Professor of Christian Formation at Denver Seminary

Jim Wilder's years of work in brain science are now paying off for all of us who have struggled with how to renew the mind for lasting transformation. I am grateful for this gigantic step in grasping the even better news of the gospel.

DUDLEY HALL, author of *Grace Works, Orphans No More*, and other books targeting spiritual growth and Christian discipleship; founder of Kerygma Ventures

Few men have seen the church as has Jim Wilder as both a theologian and psychologist. This book is a treasury offered to you. Regardless of your age you will find food for thought that you can taste and see that God is good.

JIM HYLTON, pastor, author, and conference speaker from Fort Worth, TX

I don't think I've read a more important book on discipleship in the past twenty-five years than this one. The church is starving for this book. It grows out of an understanding of the kingdom of God and impacts what that means to live it on a daily basis. This could be a game changer because it doesn't deal with the "disciplines" of discipleship as much as it does the framework of how we grow and live in community. It's not the kind of book you'll read and put down and forget—it will stay with you as you grow in the truth it teaches.

BOB ROBERTS JR., Global Senior Pastor, Northwood Church, Keller, TX; founder, Glocal.net

Every time I read a new book written by Jim Wilder, my learning curve is satisfied and blessed with teaching and tools that enable me to practice new habits and relational skills that I am eager to share with clients, friends, seminary students, identity groups, all my friends on Facebook, and everyone in the world if I could.

JOE JOHNSON, founder and director of Heart of the Father Ministries

The Other Half of Church opens a path out of the concrete structures of established churches to go into a living garden.

THOMAS GERLACH, pastor, Hagen, Germany

Michel Hendricks and Jim Wilder take you on a journey that may sound familiar—knowing biblical truths but not knowing how to genuinely live them out in relationship. What they find in wrestling with this reality leads to surprising places like combining neuroscience and early church spiritual practices. If you have a sense of dissatisfaction in your scriptural knowledge compared to your ability to live these teachings out in authentic caring relationships, read on. Michel's story is a good place to start in changing that.

FERNANDO GARZON, assistant dean, School of Psychology and Counseling, Regent University

Michel and James have dared to bring us to the realization that we have left out half of God's equation to help us grow spiritually. They scientifically and practically offer us the elements we need to engage the second half of our brain in becoming more and more Christlike for the sake of others, and bring true character transformation from the inside out—full-brained Christian character development. A must-read for all those engaged in helping others grow spiritually and for all those feeling plateaued in their own personal growth.

RANDY FRAZEE, pastor and author of *Think, Act, Be like Jesus*

For most of my Christian life (more than fifty years), I've had a nagging feeling that something important was missing when it came to spiritual growth. Jim and Michel have provided the missing piece—the critical role that my right brain plays in spiritual growth! For anyone interested in becoming a disciple or in making disciples, this book is a game changer!

JOHN WHITE, Team Leader of the LK10 Community; coauthor of *Joy Fueled: Catalyzing a Revolution of Joyful Communities*; host of the podcast *Stories from the Revolution*

Michel Hendricks and Jim Wilder have written a brilliant book that will mark a watershed moment in the lived praxis of Christian discipleship. Bridging the connections between neuroscience and the transformative power of the gospel, Hendricks and Wilder have gifted the body of Christ with profound insights into workings of the human brain in relationship to the heart of the Father for His church.

JULIA R. MOORE, Associate Professor of Religious Studies, UNC Charlotte; cofounder of Moore Grace Ministries, Charlotte, NC

The Other Half of Church clearly points out what we all know intuitively—all of our programs, classes, services, trainings, and ministries are not producing the type of transformed disciple Jesus described in John 10:10. With a winsome narrative and practical illustrations, Hendricks and Wilder give the four essential nutrients for healthy, life-changing soil. They also give practical steps toward infusing those nutrients into your life, home, community, and church. This book is essential reading for all of us who think, *There has to be more.*

TOM ANTHONY, Executive Pastor of Ministries and Outreach at Mountain Springs Church and author of *Building Better Community*

This vital and timely work takes up the challenge of learning the love that Jesus speaks to us about as life's greatest principle. It is the challenge both the individual and the church face in growing up into Christlikeness that the world desperately needs to see. The integrated approach, relating brain function to love, joy, and life, is profound. This book is a must for all serious disciples and those who disciple both in the church and in missions

BRUCE THOMPSON, Dean Emeritus, College of Counseling and Healthcare, University of the Nations, Youth with a Mission

In *The Wizard of Oz*, Scarecrow wistfully sings, "If I only had a brain . . ." The good news is that God has given us all one—a brain, that is! I invite you to read *The Other Half of Church* and consider how the Creator cares for your entire being. This book will challenge your presuppositions about how disciples are made and encourage you to avoid the sort of body versus soul dualism that has plagued the church for centuries.

TOM COX, pastor of Grace Presbyterian Church; seasoned disciple-maker and a veteran of both campus and church-based ministry

Everything you are experiencing will make much more sense when you read *The Other Half of Church*! The rest of the story that we all need to hear is that discipleship, counseling, and true change is really possible, but require us to address the whole heart, the whole mind, the whole body, and our whole self in the process!

STEVE FAIR, director, Renewal Christian Counseling Center; author, *Journey into the Divided Heart*

Michel Hendricks in his partnership with Jim Wilder has provided all of us with not only a thorough diagnosis but pathways to treatment for our most deeply rooted struggles. *The Other Half of Church* will not only help you identify why you continue to struggle to live a joyful life but it will illuminate a pathway to joy that has long been neglected.

SCOTT NICKELL, teaching pastor at Southland Christian Church in central Kentucky

The Other Half of Church is a Copernican shift in how we think and live out character transformation and spiritual and emotional growth. It is a must-read for every Christian leader, theologian, and follower of Jesus. The book is a practical guide that helps us return to long-neglected practices of Christian discipleship and how we live out the life that Jesus makes possible for all.

JOHN LAMB, professor, Colorado Christian University

The Other Half of Church may have cracked the code for what's missing in many churches today. By deftly intersecting biblical truth with neuroscience, Jim and Michel present a sound case to fertilize the soil of our churches with four biblical nutrients. By doing so, leaders can help transform the health of their churches and the hearts of their people. If you are a church leader (or not), this is a must-read book in today's increasingly uncertain times.

CHARLES STONE, PASTOR, author of *Holy Noticing: The Bible, your Brain, and the Mindful Space between Moments*

Beautifully weaving threads of theology, psychology, and neuroscience, *The Other Half of Church* brings remarkable insight into emotional maturity, spiritual formation, and healthy church community. Each page reflects timeless wisdom, guiding every longing heart down the path to the truly joyful life found in Christ and His church. This is a timely and important contribution. I highly recommend it!

TOM NELSON, senior pastor, Christ Community Church, Kansas City; president of Made to Flourish; author of *Work Matters* and *The Economics of Neighborly Love*

One of the greatest problems facing the church today is that the walk of faith and the personal lives of Christians do not go hand in hand. This is a must-read book for pastors who hope of a healthy church that Jesus envisioned, for church leaders who want to become spiritually mature, and for Christians who live a life of faith but experience no joy.

KIWON LEE, Lead Pastor of Recovery Ministry at Onnuri Community Church

I knew there was a missing ingredient in the way I was attempting to model and lift up the "Christlikeness" model, both for myself and for those with whom I was investing my life. Jim Wilder's teaching has been a guiding filter as our congregation is slowly beginning to live out what is contained in the pages of this book.

DANA HANSON, shepherd of LIFEhouse Church Los Angeles; author of *Reboot: 70 Life Lessons with Dallas Willard*

Tired of doing the little things to change your life, but what you want is lasting transformation? What we need is a full-brained Christianity that will lead us to real spiritual maturity. *The Other Half of Church* gives us just this, showing us how integrating the brain and body leads to a truly transformed life. Full of engaging stories and personal examples, the authors give a concrete picture of living a full-brained Christian life. We will be recommending this book and implementing its insights in our ministry.

CYD AND GEOFF HOLSCLAW, coauthors of *Does God Really Like Me?: Discovering the God Who Wants to Be With Us*

I believe that as the church embraces and practices the wisdom in this book, we will see a relational revolution that will equip the church for leadership training, mission, and the completion of the Great Commission. This "other half of the church" will be necessary for the immense challenges that lie ahead in our time.

WILLIAM D. (BILL) BJORAKER, Associate Professor of Judeo-Christian Studies & Contemporary Western Culture, William Carey International University

The
Other Half
of Church

Christian Community,
Brain Science, and
Overcoming Spiritual Stagnation

JIM WILDER
AND MICHEL HENDRICKS

MOODY PUBLISHERS
CHICAGO

Interior Design: Ragont Design
Cover Design: Erik M. Peterson
Cover illustration of brain art copyright © 2020 by venimo/Shutterstock (313844150). All rights reserved.
Edited by Kevin P. Emmert

Library of Congress Cataloging-in-Publication Data

Names: Hendricks, Michel, author. | Wilder, Jim, author.
Title: The other half of church : Christian community, brain science, and overcoming spiritual stagnation / Michel Hendricks and Jim Wilder.
Description: Chicago : Moody Publishers, 2020. | Includes bibliographical references. | Summary: "In The Other Half of Church, pastor Michel Hendricks and neurotheologian Jim Wilder couple brain science and the Bible to identify how to overcome spiritual stagnation by living a full-brained faith. They also identify the four ingredients necessary to develop and maintain a vibrant transformational community where spiritual formation occurs, relationships flourish, and the toxic spread of narcissism is eradicated"-- Provided by publisher.
Identifiers: LCCN 2020011241 (print) | LCCN 2020011242 (ebook) | ISBN 9780802419637 | ISBN 9780802498557 (ebook)
Subjects: LCSH: Christianity--Psychology. | Narcissism--Religious aspects--Christianity. | Thought and thinking--Religious aspects--Christianity. | Church.
Classification: LCC BR110 .H36 2020 (print) | LCC BR110 (ebook) | DDC 230.01/9--dc23
LC record available at https://lccn.loc.gov/2020011241
LC ebook record available at https://lccn.loc.gov/2020011242

Originally delivered by fleets of horse-drawn wagons, the affordable paperbacks from D. L. Moody's publishing house resourced the church and served everyday people. Now, after more than 125 years of publishing and ministry, Moody Publishers' mission remains the same—even if our delivery systems have changed a bit. For more information on other books (and resources) created from a biblical perspective, go to: www.moodypublishers.com or write to:

Moody Publishers
820 N. Lasalle Boulevard
Chicago, IL 60610

1 3 5 7 9 10 8 6 4 2

Printed in the United States of America

To Claudia, my wife: As we walk this winding road together,
I never cease to be amazed by treasure you are to me. —Michel

To my wife, Kitty, and our forty-eight years learning the ways
of her posterior cingulate cortex. —Jim

Contents

Introduction

THIS IS A STORY, not a theological term paper. I (Michel Hendricks) take you on a journey with me and my friend Jim Wilder. It is a journey that we hope will broaden your horizons about how we grow as followers of Jesus Christ. We may not wrap everything up neatly at the end, so consider this book a first step.

As the title suggests, we are explaining what is missing. *The Other Half of Church* suggests a venture into the unknown. We hope you will feel this tension throughout the book. If we want to engage in the other half, we need to be open to what has been missing. We will need to make some fundamental changes to how we have been doing things. You will be tempted to think, *That's not how we do church.*

The other half is missing, as much from our awareness as our practice. As you jump into this new material, be patient and you will find further explanation. Over the years, the saints of old have practiced the other half—they just did not know how to talk about it. And they knew nothing of its supporting structures in the magnificent design of the human brain.

I am bringing you into my own confusion as I walked into this new area of discipleship. What is missing in our Christian practice is like empty water jugs that are soon to be filled to the brim with wine of the highest quality. Before the day of the wedding at Cana, they looked like ordinary clay jugs. They were nothing special so as to attract your attention. We will introduce topics that may seem unimportant, like empty clay pots. You will understand later, and they will never seem so normal again.

You will learn that the way of healing, growth, and maturity supported in the right brain are not easily described by words. You will also find that words are dominantly left-brain products that struggle to flesh out right-brain realities. These new concepts and the accompanying practices can be learned, but patience is required. This is another ongoing tension you will encounter.

We are using a book to transmit to you something that was not intended for words on a page or from a mouth. We hate to disappoint you, but your life will not be transformed simply by reading this book. Transformation is found by engaging in the practices of the other half, some of which are described within this book. You must stick with those practices over time. This path to change will sometimes be arduous. But it is a glorious journey if you stay with it. Like a growing plant, let your roots go down and God's fruit ripen.

This is no new golden ticket to spiritual perfection. Transformation involves hard work and training. This book applies a yellow highlighter to things we have been reading in Jesus' teaching but have not been noticing. An appropriate prayer would be, "Lord, give us eyes to see what we have not seen."

1

Half-Brained Christianity

What would this idle babbler wish to say?

Acts 17:18 NASB

CLAUDIA AND I CAME home from another church feeling depressed. We were visiting churches in our area after I found myself without a job at a megachurch. I had been a discipleship pastor there, helping people grow in their Christian life. My wife and I had hoped our children would make the church we visited that day their home. Now we were skeptical. Every church we visited served the same good ideas that we had already tried but with results that disappointed us. As I set the table for lunch on our back patio, I wasn't sure I would want to attend church again.

I came out of my musing as my wife glanced at me and understood my thoughts. She set a platter of Chicken Milanesa on the table. It was a beautiful summer day, and I walked over to our tomato plants to pick a few for the salad my wife was making. The plants were taller than I was and full of tomatoes. My main job responsibility as a pastor was discipleship, to help people grow as Christians. I had hoped that the results of my ministry as a pastor would be like these plants, growing like crazy and full of fruit. Instead, the results I saw were inconsistent and often disappointing. Did I do something wrong? Maybe I was better at helping tomatoes grow than people. At least I knew how to add fertilizer to my tomatoes. To help people grow, I wasn't sure what they needed.

Meeting a Neurotheologian

When I was a pastor, I had lunch every month with two friends who were leaders in their churches. Thankfully, I was not alone in my frustration. Like me, Bob and John wanted to talk about discipleship. How do people grow? We used the phrase "spiritual formation," which is a fancy way of talking about how we become more like Jesus in our daily lives. We react to life like He does. We value what He values. We treat people the way He treats people. It is the process of "putting on the character of Christ."[1] We all agreed that this was the central task of the church. We also agreed that the church was mostly failing at this task. We were pastors and leaders, and we were admitting to each other that we were disappointed in the fruit we saw, both in our own lives and in our churches. I wasn't alone in my frustration. They had the same unanswered questions.

During one of our lunches together, Bob made a curious comment: "We need to think about the neuroscience angle of spiritual formation." Bob was in his eighties, so I thought that maybe he was having a senior moment. I ignored his comment, but a month later he said it again: "We should be careful not to neglect the role that neuroscience plays in spiritual formation."

I stopped him from continuing and said, "Bob, I have no idea what you are talking about. What do you mean?"

A smile grew on his face as he remarked, "I want to invite a friend of mine to our lunch next month. His name is Jim Wilder. I'll let him explain."

The following month, Bob invited this new man to join us. It was the day I began to discover that only half my brain was involved in learning to be a Christian.

Bob introduced our guest by saying, "This is Jim Wilder. He has a master's degree in theology and a doctorate in psychology. He calls himself a neurotheologian. He studies the intersection of spiritual formation and how our brain works."

I missed the next few minutes of conversation because I got stuck on the term *neurotheologian. Is that a word? What does it mean? Who is this man, and does he know what he's talking about?* Then I looked at him, and across the bottom of his T-shirt I read, "What is this idle babbler trying to say?" I thought, *Yes, what IS this idle babbler trying to say?* The phrase was from Acts 17, when Paul stepped into the Athens marketplace of ideas and introduced Jesus to Epicurean and Stoic philosophers. The ideas that Paul shared were so new and strange to them that they remarked, "What is this babbler trying to say?" (Acts 17:18).

Bob, John, and I had been meeting for over a year, and we were determined to leave no stone unturned in understanding how character is transformed. Could this neurotheologian understand how people grow? So when Jim asked us what we would like to know, I did not hesitate: "Explain

I was a pastor of spiritual formation, and I did not understand how people grew.

to us God's design for our brain and how this influences our growth as Christians."

He reached into his briefcase and pulled out a plastic brain.

He pulled it apart into two halves and started explaining how the human brain works. What I heard as we met over the following months startled me. Like Paul's message to the philosphers in Athens, what Jim explained about our brains was so new that I struggled to understand. Once I was able to absorb what he was saying, I realized that I was a half-brained Christian, and I was helping other Christians grow with practices that largely ignored one half of who they were. I was a pastor of spiritual formation, and I did not understand how people grew. What I was learning also explained why I grew so fast in the first eight years of my Christian faith, but little after that.

Michel's Story

What I learned from Jim about how character grows was not only relevant to my frustrating job as a pastor of discipleship, but also applicable to my own spiritual life. When I was nineteen years old, I had an encounter I can best describe as *a spiritual burst of light.* I had gone to bed one night an angst-filled young man. I was confused and lost, asking the ceiling, "What is life about? Why do I exist? What's the meaning of it all?" In the middle of the night, I had an encounter. It is hard to explain, but what I heard without words being spoken was, "I hear these questions of yours. The answer to them is My Son. He is the answer."

It was as though someone had switched on a light in my dark and confused soul. I had not been raised in a Christian family, did not attend church, and knew very little about Jesus. Hearing that He was the answer to my existential confusion was like an explosion of light and hope.

The next morning, I knew something inside me had changed. I still felt hope, which was new to me. I started reading the Bible for the first time. I became part of a community of friends who also found meaning in Jesus, the One I had encountered in the middle of that night. In the span of several months, my life looked and felt nothing like the life I had before. This was transformation! For eight years as a university student, I grew and grew. I was surrounded by people I loved and who loved me, and I saw my life change. This is the time in my life that reminded me of my tomatoes—growing like crazy and full of fruit.

Then our community began to scatter. Careers took people away as mine took me into engineering. Some married and had children. My experience of the Christian life bogged down. Growth, which for eight years seemed inevitable, became stubborn. I went through a bout of depression. I did not walk away from Jesus, but I saw much in myself that I did not like and did not know how to change. This was not the transformed life I had taken for granted. Instead, my life was often disappointing, and parts of me seemed resistant to change. My temper would flare, and it seemed beyond my control. I experienced stretches of hopelessness and spiritual lethargy. Why? Did I do something wrong? Was my church doing something wrong?

When I was the spiritual growth pastor for a megachurch, my goal was helping others experience the growth I experienced my first eight years as a Christian. In the back of my mind, I wondered whether their growth would slow like mine. Maybe this is just the way the Christian life works. Transformation starts off at a sprint and slows down to a crawl. I lowered my expectations. We talked a lot about brokenness in our church, and I found some solace there. We all are broken, but God still loves us. This is true, but I desired more. I wanted Jesus to live His life through me. I did not want an improved life. I wanted a transformed life. I found myself settling for small improvements instead of radical transformation. Why was the fruit in my church and in my life so inconsistent? Was there something lacking?

When I met Jim, I began discovering why I grew so much for eight years, and why my growth got bogged down. The details of God's design of the human brain and its role in forming character would answer the mysteries that had plagued me for thirty years. These details were unknown to humanity until recently. I was surprised by what I learned when I opened up the hood on the engine of the brain and took a look.

The Brain Discovery

Jim explained that much of what we now know about the brain has come from research in the last few decades. As the assistant director of a clinic specializing in trauma recovery, he received a flyer in the mail advertising a lecture by Dr. Allan Schore on "Affect Regulation and the Neurobiology of Attachment." The title sounded so uninteresting that Jim tried to throw the flyer away several times, but to no avail. In his words, "The flyer wouldn't fly," and he sensed that God was trying to get his attention. Jim was a busy man, so he sent an intern to find out what Dr. Schore had to say. The young man dutifully obeyed and returned on Monday, having purchased the entire set of recordings of the conference.

"This was the most boring presentation I have heard," he reported back. "Dr. Allan Schore read verbatim the contents of a manuscript he was writing. However, he talked about the ages at which the brain develops different abilities, and they matched precisely with the theory we are developing here in the clinic. So, I bought all the recordings because I didn't understand much else he was saying."

Unknown to Jim, interesting findings were coming out of UCLA where Dr. Allan Schore discovered how the human brain develops in a person through joy and attachment. Jim started attending every conference where Dr. Schore presented his material.

He was especially intrigued by a topic that Dr. Schore emphasized in all of his talks: the importance of joy for healthy brain development. Dr. Schore defined joy relationally as "someone who is glad to be with me" and "being the sparkle in someone's eye." Jim had heard little about joy while studying for his degrees in psychology and theology. *Could this be the key to unlocking the hardest cases in my practice?* he wondered. More generally, he suspected that joy and attachment might also be the keys to helping us grow as disciples of Jesus.

As Christians, we believe that God created us, including our brains. Jim explained that a fascinating aspect of God's design is that our brain is not a single unit. We have a dual processor. When you buy a cellphone, you may think that it has a single microprocessor inside controlling everything. Like the brain, that is not true. Most phones have two processors running simultaneously. One handles the cellphone communication. The second processor runs everything else. The human brain also has two processors, one on the right and another on the left, that work together but specialize in different responsibilities. This is where things get interesting. God put taste, touch, sight, smell, and hearing sensors in our bodies that help us to interpret our world. All are connected to nerves that enter the bottom of the brain. They all travel up into the brain stem and begin processing on the right side of our brain.

The Right Brain

Until this lunch, I shared the popular misconception in our culture about the left and right sides of the brain. I understood that the right side was creative and the left was analytical, and some people were left-brain dominant while others were right-brain dominant. Artists and musicians were right brained, and accountants and engineers were left brained. This was not an accurate description.

Jim explained that all of the ways in which we interpret our world, from seeing an expression on a friend's face to smelling our grandmother's roast chicken cooking in the oven, enter into our dual processor brain on the back of the right side. Processing the smell of the chicken shifts from the back to the front of the right side, and somewhere behind our right eye it crosses over to the left side. Then the smell of grandma's chicken processes from the front to the back on the left side. It is like going up one supermarket aisle and then crossing over and returning on the next aisle to the left. Everything takes this path. Words in a conversation. A handshake. A favorite song. A puzzled look on a friend's face. A math problem. The taste of grandma's chicken when you finally sit down and eat. That and everything else you experience follows this path. Back to front on the right side, front to back on the left side. As Jim explained this to us, I thought to myself, *I have never heard this before. No one has ever explained to me the basics of how the brain works.*

LEFT (SLOW TRACK)		RIGHT (FAST TRACK)
Conscious thought		Individual identity
Speech		Group identity
Strategies		Emotional attunement to others
Problem solving		
Logic		Assessment of surroundings (good, bad, scary)
Stories		
		Relational attachments

The right side starts processing our surroundings and draws conclusions before the left side is even aware of what is happening. Jim calls this "preconscious thought," meaning that our right brain processes our surroundings faster and before our conscious awareness. That was hard for me to understand, and I asked Jim to explain again. What did it mean that my right brain was processing my surroundings faster than my conscious thoughts? Jim explained it this way: "The right hemisphere process that creates our working identity integrates our reality six times per second. The brain brings together current experience and emotionally important personal memories to create an active sense of who we are in our relationships at that moment. This happens faster than we can become conscious, so we assume we just 'know' who we are at all times."

This was still hard for me to digest. I thought that my brain was filled with my conscious thoughts, but this was only half true. Much of the right half of the brain runs ahead of my conscious awareness.

"The right brain functions begin with our important relational attachments and are intended to help us be ourselves in relationships," Jim said. He calls the right side the "fast track" and the left side the "slow track." The right hemisphere is a more powerful processor than the left and samples our environment at six times a second. The left side samples at five times a second, so we often know things faster than we are conscious of them and definitely faster than we can speak about them. We might say the right brain has more horsepower. From a theological point of view, God put a lot of power into the responsibilities dominant in the right side of our brains. These functions must be important to Him and crucial to our ability to grow as disciples of Jesus.

Even as we talk about the functions of our right and left brains, we must be careful with how we explain this because of the complexity of God's design. When we think of something being located in the right brain, this layman's explanation is not technically correct. Our brains have tendrils all over both hemispheres that support the various brain functions, but the left-brain/right-brain location is where the control or unification is dominant.[2]

With that in mind, our right brain governs the whole range of relational life: who we love, our emotional reactions to our surroundings, our ability to calm ourselves, and our identity, both as individuals and as a community. The right side manages our strongest relational connections (both to people and God) and our experience of emotional connectedness to others. *And character formation.* Don't miss that. Character formation, which is a primary responsibility of the church, is governed by the right brain, not the left brain. If we want to grow and transform our character into the character of Jesus, we must involve activities that stimulate and develop the right brain.

Character formation, which is a primary responsibility of the church, is governed by the right brain, not the left brain.

Jim said the right side "tries to be sure that we can joyfully be like our people in every situation we encounter. Character is formed by answering the question, 'What would my people do now that would reflect our deepest values and maintain all our important relationships?'" He was saying that character formation develops out of our community, the people we call "my people." Our loving attachments and the values of our community drive our character. We will explain more about the importance of group identity in forming character in chapter 5.

Jim explained that our instantaneous reactions to our surroundings are created before our conscious mind is aware of them. He called them our "gut reactions and first options for response." These reactions are faster than conscious thought. Our immediate response is what we call character—how we spontaneously react to our surroundings. My discouraging job as a pastor was to help people change their character. If I wanted to help transform character, I needed to involve changing these instantaneous reactions. But I had no idea how to do that.

Being a disciple of Jesus means reacting to the world as He would react. One author describes Christian discipleship as the "way to become the kind of person who does, easily and routinely, what Jesus said—does it without having to think much about it."[3] I like that explanation, but how do we train ourselves to spontaneously act and think like Jesus if this happens faster than conscious thought?

This was hard for me to grasp because I was so accustomed to focusing on conscious activities in my Christian life—activities like praying, reading the Bible, fasting, and meditating on Scripture. Jim was opening my eyes to a vast unexplored area of growth. I had no idea that there were practices that conform my instantaneous "faster than thought" reactions to the image of Christ. I felt like I had discovered a hidden treasure.

It is likely that you are learning much of this for the first time. You might be thinking, *What does this mean practically? How do I grow spiritually if growth is governed by the right brain?* We will get to that, but the first step is to realize that *we do not grow the way we have been told.* I, in my job as a pastor of spiritual formation, had a woefully incomplete understanding of how to help people grow. In my seminary education, I was taught very little about how people grow and character is transformed. Like I was, most pastors, churches, and Christian communities are mistaken about how character is transformed. To understand how we are mistaken, let's look at the left brain.

The Left Brain

The left side of the brain is what we commonly think of as "the mind" in popular culture. Our concept of the mind describes only half of our brain. The left brain is dominant for functions we associate with the mind: logical thinking, problem solving, strategies, and language. Cause-and-effect relationships are formed here. Words are put to our life experiences to create autobiographical stories. Problems are solved. Plans are hatched. Arguments are formulated. Stories are told. Truth is defended. What we think of as "the mind" covers only one half of the brain—the left brain. The left brain runs at the speed of words; the right brain runs at the speed of joy.

God designed our left brain to understand important aspects of our Christian beliefs. Without truth we would be lost. Our beliefs and doctrine (formulated in the left brain) are created from knowing the relational love of God (formulated in the right brain). The right brain is the fast track, and it leads the left brain. This means that a smoothly running right hemisphere is necessary for our entire brain to function as designed.

Left-Brained Christianity

As John, Bob, and I listened to Jim explain the role our brain plays in spiritual formation, we looked at each other and realized, "We are half-brained Christians!" More specifically, we were left-brained Christians. We were pursuing discipleship by focusing on strategies centered on the left brain and neglecting the right brain. We were not using our full resources to help us grow to spiritual maturity. We were neglecting not only half of our brains, but also the dominant half for forming character. If we had to focus on one half of our brains in church (which we don't), we were focusing on the wrong half!

In a typical church service, we hear teaching on important truths from the Bible. At the end of the sermon, we are given an application, which usually consists of being told to make better choices. We are encouraged to trust that the Holy Spirit will give us the power to change. In small groups, we usually study questions on a Bible passage or a sermon, and at the end we discuss how to apply what we learn. Then we pray and ask God to help us. I have been taught these steps from the first day I went to church. If you are like me, you have seen this pattern in your Christian community. This is the accepted strategy for growth in Western culture, but there is one small problem. These strategies focus on half of our brain, and it is not the half that forms character. When we neglect right-brain development in our discipleship, we ignore the side of the brain that specializes in character formation. Left-brained discipleship emphasizes beliefs, doctrine, willpower, and strategies but neglects right-brain loving attachments, joy, emotional development, and identity. Ignoring right-brain relational development creates Christians who believe in God's love but have difficulty experiencing it in daily life, especially during distress. In a left-brained community we are taught Christian doctrine, but the doctrine has difficulty showing up in our instantaneous reactions:

- We are told not to lie but are not shown how to stop lying
- We are told to trust God with our money and not be greedy but are not shown how
- We believe that God loves us and that we can trust Him, yet our beliefs feel shaky when we are in distress

I am not suggesting that the familiar left-brain strategies are unimportant in discipleship. Biblical teaching, Scripture meditation, beliefs, strategies, and the choices we make play an essential role in forming our character. We don't grow without developing these left-brain skills.

However, without the proper right-brained relational and emotional environment, our fruit will be meager. When the right brain and left brain work in harmony, character transformation becomes commonplace in our communities. We are growing character in healthy soil, like the tomatoes in my backyard. I am not arguing for a right-brained Christianity instead of a left-brained Christianity, but for a full-brained Christianity.

Although this brain theologian across the table never used the term "half-brained," the shock went so deep that it has become the title of this chapter. You might think that I felt insulted or foolish sitting across the table from Jim Wilder and realizing that I was a half-brained Christian. It might sound like an insult if we confuse half-brained with harebrained. I don't believe that most Christians are harebrained, although some undoubtedly are. You might think that half-brained implies that Christians are stupid. We use only half of our brains. That is not the meaning either. Thinking about Christians and their brains was new for me. I was eager to know everything I could about how God designed our whole brain to grow us into the image of Christ.

Finding the Rest of My Brain

Contrary to the popular misconception that people are left-brain or right-brain dominant, both sides are created to operate in harmony. The right-side "fast track" leads the way. Brain scientists call this synchronization. Both sides are operating as God designed them and they are playing together nicely. A synchronized brain runs smoothly like a well-tuned engine, even under stress.

When Jim explained the technical details of right brain/left brain synchronization, I didn't understand much of what he said,[4] but I understood the importance for spiritual formation. I wanted to know more. As our lunch came to an end, Bob, John, and I asked Jim whether we could meet again. We wanted to try out some exercises that would develop our brains. Jim offered to give us a taste of what he called "relational brain skills."

A month after our lunch with John and Bob, we met again and Jim shared practices with us that train our brains to run smoothly. He showed us how to recognize when our brains have a traffic jam. He shared drills that build our joy capacity and help us handle big emotions. (You will learn more about joy in chapter 3.) He emphasized the importance of building our true identities and living in a community of belonging. When our identity is not well developed, our personality will change in different settings. With a well-formed brain, my identity will not change in different circumstances. All of these exercises help us develop and strengthen our entire brain. Even though it was unclear to me at the time how these simple exercises can form my character and emotional health, I was eager to try them. It would take me three years of practice and learning, but I have seen the results, and they look a lot like my tomato plants.

As Jim was explaining this, I thought of my job as a pastor. If I could go back and do it again, I would redesign our entire spiritual formation program. What at first sounded like theoretical brain science suddenly challenged my understanding of how we grow spiritually. Many Western Christians believe character is formed by thinking correctly, believing truth, and making wise choices in light of the truth.[5] If all of this is empowered by the Holy Spirit, we are on the path to Christian maturity. This is the philosophy I used to help people grow in their faith. I remember leading a training by saying, "To change our character, we need to change our thinking. New thinking produces new behavior." Most Christian communities agree, and it is true that correct thinking is important in discipleship. The problem is that this anthropology ignores other, more dominant drivers of character change.

Don't get discouraged if you don't understand all of the brain details. I usually need to hear explanations several times before they sink in. Much of how the brain forms character sounds strange to us. For example, a full-brained Christianity would include developing areas of our lives that are not under conscious control. Much of what we call discipleship or spiritual formation is an effort to change our spontaneous reactions to life situations and conform them to the image of Christ. Since we don't understand preconscious thought, we try consciously to change our character. This is putting the cart before the horse, since our preconscious right brain is the driver of character change, not our conscious thoughts and willpower.

The right brain integrates our life, including our connection to loved ones, our bodies, our surroundings, our emotions, our identities, and our community. Character formation flows out of these connections. The right brain processes these questions: Who is happy to see me here? What do I feel right now? Is there anyone here who understands me? How do I act like myself right now? What do my people do in this situation? The answers to these questions drive our character development.

If you are like me, you need to read that again: our right brain depends on relational input to form our character. Much of this processing is nonverbal and preconscious. Keeping our relational right brain running smoothly creates the optimum environment for character transformation. And we can train ourselves in these skills.

Neglected Soil

After hearing all of this new information about Christian growth, Claudia and I started sharing a meal with a new group of fellow Christians who were hungry to grow spiritually, like we were. Jim and his wife, Kitty, challenged our understanding of how we mature. In spite of my doubts, my understanding of how the Christian life works was being turned upside down. The group was learning and practicing something they called *hesed*, or relational brain skills. We saw glimpses of something we desired. Could this be a journey from disappointment and confusion to growth? We sensed that God was gently guiding us to reengage. Something very deep was being reawakened. I was hoping for a discipleship that was abounding in fruit instead of disappointing.

My hope for revived growth reminded me of my tomato plants. After buying our first house, I decided to plant tomatoes. To my surprise, the plants exploded over the summer, and we had hundreds of homegrown tomatoes. We had a difficult time keeping up with the harvest. I was surprised how easy and fun it was. Planting tomatoes in the spring became a yearly tradition for our family.

Unfortunately, my tomato harvest decreased over the next few years until one summer I picked only a handful. I discovered that tomatoes are heavy consumers of nutrients, so they deplete the soil over time. I was planting and watering the same way each year, but saw fewer and fewer tomatoes. My mistake was that I was neglecting the soil, which got depleted.

I read an article on the building blocks of healthy soil and immediately started building my soil back to health. I replenished the soil each year with the nutrients that tomatoes need to grow, and my harvests quickly improved. Once I met Jim and started learning more about the brain, I wondered whether the same was happening in my Christian life. Was I trying to grow in depleted soil? If so, what nutrients did my soil need? Could these nutrients be related to the new area of discipleship that Jim was sharing with us?

When I discovered the ingredients for good spiritual soil, they made sense and connected to my experience. We will see that right-brain development of relational joy, group identity, and healthy correction are essential ingredients for character transformation. We will spend a chapter studying each of these nutrients. What turned my mind upside down was their understanding of *hesed*. We will devote a chapter to this Hebrew word. I realized there was abundant *hesed* in the soil when I was growing well. Likewise, the lack of *hesed* went unnoticed when my harvest slowly dwindled. Even worse, soil without *hesed* favored the growth of weeds. We will look at a specific weed that grows in poor soil in a later chapter.

I am going to take you on my journey of discovery. We will learn to maintain healthy soil that supports bountiful growth. This trek might make you stop dead in your tracks and wonder, *Is this too good to be true?* Other times, the new perspectives may seem confusing and even overwhelming. This adventure has caused me to reinterpret my own life and my experiences as a pastor. My understanding of church and how people grow was turned upside down. This journey will likely have you rethinking many assumptions you have about spiritual formation and especially how we grow.

As Claudia and I continued to meet on Sunday afternoons with our new group of friends, we embarked on an intriguing adventure. Much of what we learned went against the tide of our previous Christian experience. We began feeling the flow of life-giving nutrients. We started seeing spontaneous changes in our character, much like I saw in my first years of faith. I even saw growth in my stubborn areas that seemed resistant to change. We were so excited that we talked to anyone who would listen. My wife lamented that we hadn't learned this years ago. We have grown more in the last two years than in the last twenty. This is our impetus for sharing our story with anyone who hungers.

In the next chapter, we will discover how many churches adopted the flawed model of discipleship I used as a pastor. We will learn how our soil became depleted and what steps we can take to replenish the nutrients. The church did not start out being half-brained. In the book of Acts we find a vibrant whole-brained community. But several hundred years ago, culture changes[6] pulled the Christian faith toward practices that are left-brain dominant.[7] Growing disciples of Jesus became focused primarily on thoughts, words, strategies, and arguments for truth. Relational skills and maturity were largely neglected. The results have been disastrous for our relational soil.

Unfortunately, the consequences of half-brained Christianity do not stop at anemic character change. Something dark grows in Christian community when the soil loses its nutrients. I was to discover that narcissism thrives in depleted soil, especially in positions of leadership. Headlines are filled with the downfall of pastors and leaders, devastating churches, ministries, and families. A whole-brained Christianity creates communities that are both transformational and resistant to narcissism.

- -

When we fail to engage the full brain in our Christian communities, our spirituality gravitates to a left-brained Christianity. We lose the relational and emotional skills that form our character. Without them, our discipleship is ineffective. Left-brained Christianity not only leads to a lack of character growth, it creates a relational environment that is optimal for narcissism to flourish.

- -

GROUP DISCUSSION QUESTIONS

1. Do you relate to Michel's surprise at discovering he was a left-brained Christian?
2. Are the spiritual practices you have been taught mostly left-brained, right-brained, or a good mix of the two (whole-brained)?
3. Discuss what your life might be like with more right-brained focused skills: more joy, a better ability to regulate distressing emotions, a more coherent identity, and the ability to feel God's face shining on you.
4. Does the soil of your Christian community have signs of being depleted? How common is transformation in your church?

2

How Do People Grow?

So Christ himself gave the apostles, the prophets, the
evangelists, the pastors and teachers, to equip his people
for works of service, so that the body of Christ may
be built up until we all reach unity in the faith and in
the knowledge of the Son of God and become mature,
attaining to the whole measure of the fullness of Christ.

Ephesians 4:11–13

I BECAME A PASTOR in a roundabout way. I did not aim
my career toward ministry. I had a corporate job doing something
I enjoyed. I started going to seminary part time, but not with the
intent of becoming a pastor. Hunger was my motivation. I wanted
more than I was receiving from my church. I took my time, taking
two classes a semester. I completed my three-year degree (if done
full time) in eleven years. The president of the seminary joked
about my longevity during the graduation ceremony. I loved
seeing nuances in the New Testament in Greek. My eyes were

opened by studying the growth of Christianity around the world. Knowing more about God and the Bible satisfied my hunger. Still, it left me wanting more character change. My knowledge and understanding had increased, but my character had not improved as much as I had hoped.

Over time, I became more involved in a growing church, eventually as a part of the leadership. I was asked to join the elder team and I became friends with many of the pastors and elders. While attending an intense men's weekend with several pastors, I felt connected and encouraged in a way that I had not for many years. During that weekend, we worked on the darkest experiences of our past with the support of other men. They looked us in the eyes and blessed us. I was deeply moved.

Almost immediately, my pastor started recruiting me. "Why not quit your job and do this for a living with our church?" The "this" he was talking about was discipleship. Our church lacked a plan for spiritual growth. We were good at getting people into an auditorium and giving them a taste of the love and grace of Jesus. We were scattered and unfocused when it came to the next steps.

The title of this chapter came from a question I often asked God as the pastor of spiritual formation. I wanted to help our people grow as Christians. When I saw the crowds streaming into the lobby of our church, I wondered, *How do I help these people grow and mature?* I also asked the question of myself.

I had the privilege of creating my own job description, and I leaned on two Scriptures for help. The first was Matthew 28:18–20. These words were particularly interesting because they were the last commands Jesus gave His closest friends. This commission was left ringing in the disciples' ears after Jesus handed them the keys of the church and left earth. He was reminding them of their primary responsibility as His chosen leaders. He said,

"All authority in heaven and on earth has been given to me. Therefore go and make disciples of all nations, baptizing them in the name of the Father and of the Son and of the Holy Spirit, and teaching them to obey everything I have commanded you. And surely I am with you always, to the very end of the age."

Over the centuries, these words were given a title, "the Great Commission," that clearly states the mission Jesus gave the leaders of His church: go and make disciples.

According to Jesus, disciple making has two steps. The first step is to baptize people. Jesus is using a literary device where he is wrapping up the process of evangelism into one word. This first step, baptizing, includes talking to our friends about Jesus and telling them our experience of His love. We invite them into our communities, our churches, our homes. We love them. We give them a taste of God's kingdom and share the good news of the hope we have in Jesus.

When God opens the eyes of their hearts to His love and salvation, a miracle happens. They are saved! They enter into a relationship meant to be so transformational that they become new creatures (see 2 Cor. 5:17). We celebrate salvation with a vivid sacrament. Baptism is a symbol that we died and rose again from the grave (see Rom. 6:4). We have a brand-new life. In the Great Commission, Jesus combines this whole process into the word *baptize*. This is the first step of discipleship.

The second step in the Great Commission is to teach people to obey everything Jesus has commanded us. If you mistakenly think that Jesus' commission only applied to the original disciples, the apostle Paul repeats the second step in Ephesians 4:12–13. Paul's restatement is the other Scripture I used to form my job description. Paul specifically directs this teaching to leaders—apostles, prophets, evangelists, pastors, and teachers. Their central responsibility is to "equip his people for works of service, so that the body of Christ may be built up until we all reach unity in the faith and in the knowledge of the Son of God and become mature, attaining to the whole measure of the fullness of Christ."

In this second step, leaders help their people grow to maturity. Jesus and Paul expect the long slow work of character formation. The goal of discipleship, when it fulfills its purpose, is maturity. Any discipleship process that does not bring a person to maturity has failed to achieve its goal. Christian leaders direct their people in the process of spiritual formation until they become "people who have the character of Christ."[1]

I saw the Great Commission as my job description. It gave me the "what" but not the "how." I still needed an answer to the question in the title of this chapter: How do people grow? As a pastor I would sit in my office and ponder that question. Do I just tell people what to do? Do I give them a list of the dos and don'ts? Does everyone just need the right information? I quickly found out that information alone was insufficient.

In spite of my unanswered question, I did my best to follow Paul's teaching in Ephesians 4:11–13. I started developing a path for the people in our church to grow to maturity. My first step was writing a short book on the basics of the Christian faith. We had many brand-new Christians in our community. Many of them had never read a single book of the Bible. They reminded me of myself when I first became a Christ follower. I wanted to give them an accessible introduction to the basics, so I called my book *Basic Training for Walking with Jesus*.[2] I made it easy to read. When I was a new Christian, people often used religious words that I did not understand. I was careful to explain words before using them and assumed no prior knowledge of the Bible. We handed out more than 20,000 copies, and the feedback was encouraging.

For example, one man wrote to me saying that while reading *Basic Training*, his young daughter sat down next to him. He was surprised when she asked, "Daddy, would you read this book to me?" A few chapters in, she said, "Daddy, I want to follow Jesus. Can you help me become a Christian?" I heard many stories like that. The results were encouraging. My little book helped people grow. *Sometimes.*

Basic Training often helped people gain a stronger grasp of God's love and the new life Jesus offers. Other times, it didn't seem to work at all. Sometimes people who had read *Basic Training* would act as if they had not read it. For example, I wrote a chapter on forgiveness and how all of our sins have been forgiven in Christ—past, present, and future. Often, people who had read the book struggled to believe God had forgiven the horrible things they had done. When I pointed out Scriptures that clearly taught that God forgives us, it did not seem to help them. They needed something more. If I evaluate my book, I would say that it worked really well sometimes. The word *sometimes* began to bother me as a pastor. Why does this work sometimes?

Dallas Willard and the Great Omission

In my search for answers, I devoured the books of Dallas Willard. You may not be familiar with him, but Willard taught and wrote extensively on the importance of transformation and discipleship in the Christian life. Willard believed that spiritual formation is the central task of the local congregation, the primary responsibility that Jesus gave Christian leaders.[3] Our job as pastors, first and foremost, is to build the character of Jesus into people's lives. We focus on changing people on the inside. Since our inner character transformation drives everything else we do, discipleship must be central.

Willard believed that spiritual formation is the central task of the local congregation, the primary responsibility that Jesus gave Christian leaders.

Unfortunately, when he looked at churches, he noted a pattern of neglect. Spiritual formation was pushed to the side by leaders who focused on other priorities and projects. When this happened, character formation became ineffective, watered down, or dropped altogether. Christian leaders often did not take character transformation seriously. Poor character was the elephant in the church no one wanted to acknowledge.[4] Willard believed that obedience comes from inner character transformation, what he called "the renovation of the heart." In his opinion, disappointingly few hearts were being renovated.

The lack of discipleship was so widespread that Willard labeled this failure "the Great Omission."[6] He had a good sense of humor and was making a play on words with the Great Commission. When he looked at the Great Commission and then looked how churches were trying to fulfill it, Willard concluded that most were focused on the first step and ignored or watered down the second step. Churches were trying to reach lost people with the good news of Jesus. Once people were saved, they were left in permanent spiritual kindergarten without a path to maturity. The modern church "aims to get people into heaven rather than to get heaven into people."[6] Many pastors and leaders are not taking the second step of the Great Commission seriously.

Dallas Willard's mission was to put discipleship back at the center of church where it belongs. He believed that leaders must become "possessed" by the importance of discipleship. There are many good things pastors *can* do, but discipleship is the one thing pastors *must* do. All other activities and programs work best when they flow from a robust maturity formed through discipleship. When discipleship becomes the *"exclusive primary goal* of the local congregation,"[7] everything a church accomplishes is done in the character of Christ.

Willard urged churches to create a "curriculum for Christlikeness," a well-designed, intently pursued path to maturity.[8] Everyone in a Christian community should receive robust discipleship training. He encouraged readers to ask their pastors something like, "What is your plan for teaching our people to do everything Christ commanded?"

Every group that takes its purpose seriously trains their people. The military uses basic training that incoming civilians must endure in order to become soldiers. Every professional sports team has a specific and rigorous training program to turn amateurs into professional athletes. Most churches have no such program; this is "the great omission."

As I read Willard's books, I still wondered, *How? How does a church provide a path to maturity? How do we help people change? How is a heart renovated?* His answer was *spiritual disciplines.* He said, "Disciplines are activities that *are* in our power and that enable us to do what we cannot do by direct effort."[9] A simple list of spiritual disciplines would include Scripture meditation, solitude, silence, fasting, prayer, service, and celebration. As we make spiritual disciplines a part of our intentional daily practices, they will change us from the inside out. The changes we see may be slow and involve hard work. But over time, we expect fundamental changes in our character.

After reading about spiritual disciplines, I immediately went to work. I created a Bible reading plan for everyone in our church. I also started training people in spiritual disciplines. During the five-week training, everyone had a chance to practice. We focused on different disciplines each week, and I helped them unpack their experiences. By the end of five weeks, they had practiced nine spiritual disciplines.

Over six hundred people went through the training, and the results were encouraging. One woman commented after the last week, "I had no idea this type of work existed in the church. Thank you for creating this!" Another man credited the training with saving his marriage. I was encouraged because people were growing. *Sometimes.*

There's that word again. If I'm honest, my results with disciplines were mixed. Some people were blown away by the changes they saw in their lives. Other people seemed resistant, almost impervious. Something was missing. The results were inconsistent, and I wondered why. My quest to understand transformation still had missing pieces. I kept wondering and praying. *How do I help people grow?* Why don't I see more character transformation? It was around this time that I first had lunch with Jim Wilder. God answered my prayers.

The Brain and Discipleship

When Jim Wilder explained to Bob, John, and me how the brain works, we learned that character change requires full-brain engagement. I realized the materials and trainings I created for my church leaned heavily toward the left brain. I overlooked the dominant side for character change, the right brain. Jim believes that right-brain relational skills should be among the first things we teach new believers because this is the pattern we see in Jesus' life. Our love for Jesus (a right-brain attachment function) is what produces obedience. We see an example of this in John 14:22–24:

Then Judas (not Judas Iscariot) said, "But, Lord, why do you intend to show yourself to us and not to the world?"

Jesus replied, "Anyone who loves me will obey my teaching. My Father will love them, and we will come to them and make our home with them. Anyone who does not love me will not obey my teaching."

Notice the order. Judas wonders why Jesus doesn't reveal Himself to everyone. Jesus says that He reveals Himself only to those who love Him. Love is the first step. We love Jesus, and we will obey. When we do not love Jesus, we will not obey Him. We will see in later chapters that our loving attachment to Jesus forms our character. A left-brain view of Jesus' teaching would conclude that we need to choose to obey, and this will prove that we love Him. This is exactly backwards. If I want to obey Jesus, I need to focus on right-brain skills that help me love Him and receive His love. My behavior will then take care of itself. Our brains are designed to change us through love.

The development of our relational and emotional life helps our soil be more fruitful while the spiritual disciplines remove obstacles to our growth. If I lack right-brain relational development, the spiritual disciplines will be less effective. Even healthy seeds will not grow well in depleted soil.

Now we see the common problem in churches, even when taking the Great Commission seriously. We often focus on building our "personal relationship with Jesus" yet fail to integrate people into a community.[10] Full-brained discipleship contains both. Half-brained Christianity emphasizes left-brained skills (truth, doctrine, teaching, evangelism skills, ministry strategies) and neglects right-brain relational and emotional skills. A full-brained discipleship maintains both in balance.

When Christian leaders do not train people in love, relational skills, and identity, this neglect produces a half-baked disciple-ship. Most leaders, like me, have never developed their own maturity skills. Churches are filled with leaders who are gifted at theology, preaching, and vision-casting, but may not have relational and emotional skills. Negative headlines reveal their prevalence in ministry.

Dallas Willard wrote that pastors often focus on less important tasks and push aside the most important job of discipleship. This is a natural result of left-brained Christianity, which gravitates toward strategies that are measurable—number of dollars, number of people, number of campuses, number of small groups. The slow, messy work of character formation, which is hard to measure, is displaced by quantifiable goals.

If we try to measure the progress of Jesus' ministry over three years, the numbers would be disappointing. Yet Jesus never took His eyes off of His primary responsibility. He spent three years building up the character of twelve young men. If you are wondering whether discipleship is easy to measure, look at the results of these three years. Even for the Son of God, the results were often messy and disappointing. Jesus was teaching them how to live in the kingdom of God on earth, and this is hard to plug into a spreadsheet.

Dallas Willard affirmed my reality when he observed that discipleship in the church often gets watered down or ignored. Jim Wilder would add a third possibility. Our discipleship can also be ineffective because it is left-brain dominant instead of full brained. Left-brain discipleship explains the inconsistency I saw as a pastor of spiritual formation. Practices seemed to work for some people but not for others. What I realized later was that the people who did not respond to training likely had right-brain obstacles: low joy, isolation, a lack of loving community, poor identity formation, and unhealed trauma. Each of these was a relational/emotional problem requiring right-brain development. As a pastor, I did not realize that these obstacles even existed. I was ignorant of relational skills and could offer my people encouragement, prayer, Scripture, and spiritual disciplines. For some, it worked well; for others, not at all.

Let's compare the experiences of Greg and Chris. Greg was a new Christian who had never read the Bible. I put him on our Bible reading plan, and I started meeting with him monthly. I told him to bring any questions he had to our meeting, and I would do my best to give him answers. His reading progress was up and down. Some months, he was excited and had lots of questions. Other times, he sheepishly admitted that he hadn't done the reading. I showed him grace and told him that this is normal but not to give up. Not only did he not give up, but he grabbed three friends and they all jumped on the plan together. After six months, he had read through the entire New Testament for the first time in his life. He commented, "Now, in church, when the pastor teaches on a Scripture, I realize that I already know that verse! I am surprised by how different I feel after reading the Bible every day."

Similarly, I met with Chris. Unlike Greg, Chris grew up in a Christian family. When I realized that he did not know much of the Bible, I asked whether he would like to try the spiritual discipline of Scripture study. I challenged him to start our Bible reading plan. The reaction on his face surprised me. He looked like I was challenging him to endure torture. I also detected shame, even though I was happy to do it with him. He started to distance himself from me, and I wondered what had happened. Later, he shared several bad experiences he had with Christian leaders pressuring him "to do things." He had a block with reading the Bible. I did not know how to handle that. Nothing in my seminary education prepared me for this problem.

Chris had a low level of joy and painful memories of being

pressured to read the Bible. Memories tripped up his right-brain processing when I challenged him to start a Bible reading plan. I offered him spiritual disciplines but ignored developing his heart. I set him up for failure. We will see in the next chapter that when joy is low, our brain is not in a state that responds well to spiritual practices, including reading the Bible.

As a pastor, I offered a full suite of left-brain strategies. I didn't know that right-brained skills existed. This explained the inconsistent results I saw in my church. I offered:

- Resources to help people learn theology (a predominantly left-brained activity)
- I promoted a plan to help people study the Bible (a predominantly left-brained activity)
- I created a training to help people use spiritual disciplines to help them grow (mostly left-brain-centered disciplines, although some are unintentionally right-brained disciplines, too)

These spiritual disciplines are important. Yet we will soon discover that fruit will be inconsistent when there is:

- Low joy
- Shallow relational attachments
- Unstable identity
- Weak community

I began to meet with Jim more frequently. We talked about the theory of how people change, and I tried out some right-brain skills. As I began practicing these new exercises, I realized why spiritual disciplines worked sometimes and not others. If we take into account the right brain, the mystery clears up. My training had neglected an important area of spiritual growth, and, as a result, my people had not been nurtured according to the way God designed the human brain.

The Start of the Problem

With my questions about how God designed us to grow and why so many churches see so little character transformation answered, I turned to finding out how we got here. Over the last four hundred years, the cultural ground around the church has shifted. Philosophical developments from the Enlightenment altered the way we looked at ourselves as humans. The mind was elevated to be the most important part of our humanity. This emphasis on thinking and reasoning created an environment where knowledge and science flourished, with many benefits for humanity. However, many Christians began seeing themselves as mostly a mind, or as James K. A. Smith has coined it, "brains-on-a-stick."[11] Perhaps we should say "half a brain on a stick."

Some pastors and leaders saw this philosophical shift as a threat to God's authority. Reason and skepticism replaced God's Word as the path to knowledge and fulfillment. However, many Christian thought leaders agreed that our minds were the most important aspect of our humanity.[12] Christianity followed Enlightenment culture and slowly became focused on correct thinking. The importance of teaching people to love by creating loving communities was neglected. In this new world, it became more important to be right than loving. The proliferation of denominational splits and the ongoing failure of Christian leaders point to an overreliance of espousing right beliefs and neglecting maturity. If you haven't experienced people in church being right at the expense of being loving, you haven't been paying attention.

Without an awareness of the brain's role in forming identity,

Christian leaders gravitated toward left-brain strategies and neglected right-brain loving attachments. Discipleship became unbalanced. Christians thought of themselves as people with the right answers. Truth and choice became the recipe to get into heaven. Pastors primarily prepared for preaching positions through education, not character formation. Like their pastors, most Christians possessed truth, but weren't trained how to love well.[13]

The Industrial Revolution intensified the problem by breaking down the relational bonds that held families and communities together. The last several centuries produced a society that is less relationally connected. Multiple generations no longer lived and grew old in the same towns. Grandparents now visited their grandchildren several times a year instead of being integrated into their upbringing. Parents worked outside the home. Children grew up in childcare facilities and schools. Families seldom worked together. Watching screens increasingly dominated our relaxation time, replacing face-to-face interaction. Right-brain dominant relational skills were slowly being lost. The practices that transmit these emotional and relational skills have been interrupted. Culture was losing its full-brained relational skills as the church followed along.

Dallas Willard the Prophet

I saw the effects of this relational breakdown in churches where I was involved. Often I felt like I was swimming against the current trying to keep character formation as our central task. "Bigger and better" was like a siren call to abandon the messy work of discipleship, developing relational skills, and pursuing inner transformation. I saw leaders being swayed by the appeal of bigger meetings, more campuses, and more small groups. These goals were not bad in themselves, but they were accompanied by an unstated change in priorities. Discipleship, which these churches once championed, was slowly pushed off to the side and watered down. Eventually, spiritual formation was de-resourced and discontinued. The great omission triumphed again.

Dallas Willard was prophetic. He wrote about the tendency for churches to lose interest in discipleship. In *Renovation of the Heart*, he wrote that the survival and success of the institution becomes the priority instead of spiritual formation. "Discipleship to Christ is either dropped altogether," he writes, "or is redefined as devotion to the institution."[14] Even if a church gives lip service to spiritual formation, too often leaders are not willing to do the hard work it involves. After all, if we are changed by information (good sermons and Bible studies), why put effort into spiritual formation that is slow and messy? Pastors and elders often feel pressure to get fast results that look impressive. Discipleship does not excite a leader whose eyes are fixed on numbers. Dallas saw this so often that he once complained to a friend that many people were reading his books and talking about spiritual formation, but few were actually doing it.

In modern thinking, character is transformed by truth, correct thinking, and good choices. However, this formula does not translate into character formation. I do not want to imply that truth and choice are unimportant. The error is believing that thinking (by itself) forms character. What started with an elevated view of the human mind has developed into the great omission. This failure of our churches is a natural result of half-brained Christianity. We now see how philosophical[15] and anthropological priorities in the last four hundred years have led to an endemic lack of character transformation in the Western church.[16]

Soil

It might sound like a humiliating experience for me to realize I was a half-brained Christian. Admittedly, I was a pastor in charge of helping people grow who didn't know how to help them. I can see how that might be embarrassing. Quite the contrary, I was elated. When I realized that my training was ignoring half of my brain, I also realized that there was an entire half of my brain just sitting there waiting to be trained! I finally had answers to the puzzling inconsistency I saw in myself and others. The neuroscience of character transformation taught me to use my entire brain. I was excited to experience a full-brained faith and eager to share it with others.

As of the writing of this book, my wife and I have been practicing right-brain skills for two years. I will explain our training in a later chapter, but the results we see in our lives are surprising in a particular way: I find myself spontaneously acting more like Jesus, without even thinking about it. I am growing again like I did my first eight years as a Christian.

This book is not about the specifics of our training[17] but rather the relational environment required for training to work. I am writing about relational soil. Many churches and families are trying to grow in depleted soil. The relational nutrients are run down and exhausted. In order to find out how the great omission becomes the Great Commission again, we will look at the four building blocks of healthy soil. When these four nutrients are missing, we see shriveled, fruitless plants. There is little transformation, because the parts of our brain that work to grow our character are malnourished and underdeveloped. Like in my tomato garden, healthy soil is essential for vibrant growth.

Not all growth is good. There is a relational disease that spreads like a weed in depleted soil. We must examine an invasive weed in the church, and you may wonder why. What do weeds have to do with character growth? We will see that the four ingredients so essential for Christlike character, when absent, present the ideal soil for growing narcissism. Left-brain communities not only produce meager character growth, but produce a garden where narcissism thrives and spreads. Half-brained churches and families end up growing the wrong thing. I see a surprising opportunity here. The same soil needed for character growth is simultaneously resistant to narcissism.

The four ingredients so essential for Christlike character, when absent, present the ideal soil for growing narcissism.

As in my garden, the place we start improving the harvest is in the soil. Fortifying the soil of our Christian communities will involve rethinking our way of living. In the next chapter we will look at the first ingredient—the often misunderstood concept of joy.

When we fail to understand how people grow, we lose track of the central task Jesus gave the church. Having no plan for transformation produces Christians with poor character who try to do good ministry. Jesus did the opposite. He started His ministry by preaching about a transformed inner life that drives the outer life. A transformed inner life then drives everything we do.

GROUP DISCUSSION QUESTIONS

1. Have you ever attended a church that had a well-developed intentional plan to build your maturity?

    a. If so, what worked and did not work?

    b. If not, why do you think a maturity plan was absent?

2. Read Matthew 28:18–20.

    a. Up to now, how did you think we learn to obey everything Jesus commanded?

    b. How have you taught others to obey?

3. Read Ephesians 4:11–13.

    a. How have you been built up to maturity as a Christian?

    b. Who equipped you (over the years) as your spiritual leaders on your path to maturity?

3

- - - - - - - - -

Joy:
The Face of Jesus
That Transforms

For God, who said, "Let light shine out of darkness," made
his light shine in our hearts to give us the light of the
knowledge of God's glory displayed in the face of Christ.

2 Corinthians 4:6

WHEN I FIRST encountered Jesus in the middle of the night as
a nineteen-year-old, I felt a mixture of hope and excitement. I also
felt a presence like a warm emotional light. The excitement was
not only mine but His. I could feel that Jesus was excited about
what had just happened between us. I cannot prove this because
it was all nonverbal. He spoke no audible words to me. I had only
read six chapters of the New Testament, so I had little biblical
basis for anything I was feeling. I simply felt that Jesus was happy
and smiling at me, and it felt like a warm light shining on me.

When I woke up the next morning, I still felt the light. I had a summer job in downtown Denver delivering blueprints on a bicycle. As I went through my day, I was in a heightened state of spiritual awareness and excitement. I felt like I was floating ten feet above my bicycle seat. I rode past a light pole that had a sticker on it that read, "Jesus loves you!" I had ridden by this same pole every day that summer, but I had never seen the sticker before. I couldn't stop the words from coming out of my mouth: "I agree! Jesus loves me!" I had been a Christian for only seven hours, and I was already enjoying the first ingredient of healthy soil.

Over the following year, my Bible reading led me to 2 Corinthians 4:6, which gave me words for my experience: "For God, who said, 'Let light shine out of darkness,' made his light shine in our hearts to give us the light of the knowledge of God's glory displayed in the face of Christ." Even today, when I read this verse, it takes me back to that night. This is what I felt when I met Jesus. I felt the light of His face shining on me. I could feel it in my body.

If Dr. Schore is right about the definition of joy being what I feel when I see the sparkle in someone's eye that conveys "I'm happy to be with you," I was experiencing joy. Jesus' eyes were sparkling at me. His face was shining on me, and I could feel it. I wondered whether this was what it felt like to be a Christian. As far as I knew, none of my friends were Christians, so I had no one to ask.

Joy was new to me because I did not grow up in a Christian family. My parents did not take us to church or talk about God. When our family visited my grandmother in Nebraska, she would take us to her small church on Sunday mornings. I did not feel joy there. These visits were my only exposure to church.

For the rest of the summer, I continued reading the New Testament to learn more about Jesus, and I kept feeling Him smiling at me. As my summer came to an end, I moved back to the university for my sophomore year. I was unpacking my suitcase in my dorm room when Steve Lo walked in, set his two suitcases on the floor, and said, "Before I unpack, I need to talk to you."

Steve and I had become friends as freshmen, and we decided to room together our sophomore year. He continued, "Last year we partied a lot and got drunk, but I'm a Christian. Over the summer, I decided that I'm not going to do that anymore. You might not want to live with me this year. I'm not going to party with you. I'm done with that."

As soon as I heard Steve say that he was a Christian, I ignored everything else he said and waited for him to stop talking. As soon as I got my chance, I blurted out, "I'm a Christian, too!" I remember the stunned look on his face as I told him about my encounter with Jesus in the middle of the night.

I had been reading Matthew for a month, and I did not understand much of what I read. I had a thousand questions, so Steve sat down, and we talked for two hours. He knew a lot more about the Bible and walking with Jesus than I did. After I couldn't think of any more questions to ask, Steve said, "We should find a Christian group here on campus and meet some other Christians."

I did not know what a Christian group was or did, but we found one and got involved. I heard the students in this group call it a ministry. I didn't know what that word meant. They talked about evangelism. I didn't know that word, either. They used a lot of words I didn't know. They also sang songs that were strange to my musical ears. I liked the people, though, and quickly got into a small group. Within a few weeks, I was studying the Bible with new friends, and they taught me the basics about being a disciple of Jesus. They taught me how to study the Bible, how to pray and how to share my faith. One thing I wasn't taught was the importance of joy and relational attachments. I wasn't taught it, but I was shown it.

I lived a very different life that year compared to my freshman year. We talked about Jesus all the time. We prayed for each other. We did homework and ate meals together. Once a semester we prayed all night long. We had a weekly meeting, and when I showed up, I could feel that I belonged. Faces lit up when I walked into the room. My face lit up too, and it felt similar to what I experienced with Jesus. This was joy, but I did not know it at the time.

Joy and the Neglected Face of God

I thought back on these experiences in college as we continued meeting with Jim Wilder and learned about the importance of joy. I was fascinated and decided to learn all I could. I found out from Jim and others that God designed our brains to run on joy like a car runs on fuel. Jim said, "Our brains desire joy more than any other thing." As we go through our day, our right brains are scanning our surroundings, looking for people who are happy to be with us.

I read through the Bible looking for joy, and I found it everywhere. I already shared that 2 Corinthians 4:6 talks about the light of God shining in the face of Jesus. Numbers 6:24–26 is a blessing that God taught to Israel. It became a regular prayer of blessing for the Jewish nation.

> "The LORD bless you
>   and keep you;
> the LORD make his face shine on you
>   and be gracious to you;
> the LORD turn his face toward you
>   and give you peace."

When I read "the LORD make his face shine on you" and "the LORD turn his face toward you," this sounded like the neurological definition of joy. This blessing falls under the definition of joy that

Dr. Schore discovered from his research on the brain. We don't know his beliefs, but the professor was discovering what God knew all along. God designed our brains for joy, and He wants us to live in the glow of His delight. This blessing expresses a joy that can be paraphrased, "May you feel the joy of God's face shining on you because He is happy to be with you!"[1]

Joy is both misunderstood and neglected in the modern church. Jim mentioned that in his many years of education in theology and psychology, he was never taught about the importance of joy. I have a master's degree from a seminary and was never exposed to more than a rote explanation of joy. One reason for the lack of a coherent theology of joy is word choices translators make in some Bible versions. When translating the original languages of the Bible, joy sometimes disappears in modern languages. We see it clearly in the Hebrew, but it gets lost in translation. An example is Psalm 89:15. The NIV translates this, "Blessed are those who have learned to acclaim you, who walk in the light of your presence, LORD." In the Hebrew, "in the light of your presence" is literally "in the light of your face." This is not an isolated example. Over and over I discovered the neglected face of God.

God's face is connected with joy in the Bible. One of the first Scriptures I memorized when I was a new Christian was Psalm 16:11, "In Your presence is fullness of joy" (NASB). However, the original Hebrew renders this verse, "abundance of joy with your face." Psalm 21 lists the blessings of God for the king of Israel. In verse 6, the psalmist proclaims, "You make him joyful with gladness in Your presence" (NASB). The word-for-word rendering of the Hebrew is, "You make him happy with joy with your face." In Scripture, we see that the face of God brings us joy, but God's face gets erased in translation.

Some versions of the Bible alter the image of God's face shining on us, presenting a more generic concept of God's presence and favor. Translators may do this to make the text more readable, but an important bodily sensation is lost. "The light of God's presence" does not feel the same in our bodies as "the light of God's face." God designed facial recognition circuitry into our brains and linked it to our joy center. My wife's face lights up when she sees me, and this initiates a joyful chain reaction in my brain that I can feel in my body.

Brain science reveals that this joy sensation is crucial for emotional and relational development. Our brain looks specifically to the face of another person to find joy, and this fills up our emotional gas tank. The face is key. When a Bible translation erases the picture of God's face, our brains do not react as strongly. A right-brain dominant relational sensation (joy—God's face shining on us) is replaced with a less corporeal statement of fact (God is present with us). They both are important aspects of God's love for us, but they are not the same.

This may seem like nitpicking, but there is a difference in the way our bodies respond. God designed our brains to seek joy through eyes and facial expressions, through being with people who are glad to be with us. When I compared the many Scriptures that describe God's face shining on us with what I now know about how our brains were designed, I came to three important points of convergence: (1) Joy is primarily transmitted through the face (especially the eyes) and secondarily through voice. (2) Joy is relational. It is what we feel when we are with someone who is happy to be with us. Joy does not exist outside of a relationship. (3) Joy is important to God and to us.

Reading through the Bible and replacing "joy" with the concept of God's face lighting up gives us a better idea of what joy means and how it feels in our bodies. For example, if we rewrite Psalm 16:11 using the fuller definition of joy, "In Your presence is fullness of joy" becomes "When Your face lights up because You are so happy to be with me, You fill me up with joy!" In John 15, Jesus talks about how He loves His disciples with the same love that the Father has for Him. Then He says, "I have told you this so that my joy may be in you and that your joy may be complete" (v. 11). If we replace "joy" with the fuller definition, Jesus' statement would be, "My Father's face lights up when He sees Me because I'm so special to Him. I'm telling you this so that you will feel how special you are to my Father and to Me. Our faces are shining on you with delight." I can feel that in my body when I picture it. Can you?

Losing Our Bodies

Another reason joy is disregarded is that we often neglect bodily sensations in our modern Christian practice. This happens not only with the word *joy*; it represents a general trend. Words that are strongly connected to sensations in our bodies are translated in ways that are more cerebral and conceptual. For example, when Jesus is walking down the road and hears two blind men crying out to him for healing, we read that He "had compassion on them" (Matt. 20:34). The word *compassion* comes from a Greek verb that means "to be moved in one's intestines or guts." Jesus saw these blind men pleading for help, and His stomach ached with compassion. Compassion is felt in our bodies just like joy. The disconnection of our bodies from our experience of God is a direct consequence of half-brained Christianity.

The right hemisphere is where the internal and spatial sensations of our body are brought together and coordinated, giving us what one researcher calls "an integrated sense of the body."[2] Our right brain governs our emotions and awareness of our bodies. In times of distress, low joy, or general left-brained dominant living, this integration dims or breaks down. We will often feel "outside our bodies" or "in our minds." In left-brained Christianity, we tend to lose our sense of feeling God's presence in our body. The right brain governs this ability, so as we gravitate toward a full-brained discipleship, we grow to experience God in our bodies. We believe that God designed our bodies to feel and enjoy Him.

Experiencing God in my body was a foreign concept to me when I first encountered this teaching. I remember asking Jim, "What am I supposed to feel?" He responded that different people feel God's joy in different ways. What is important is that we are aware of something. Butterflies on our skin. Electricity going up the back of our neck. A tightness in our gut. A sense of warmth or lightness. Feeling joy in our bodies indicates that our right brain is functioning smoothly. When we lose this bodily connection, it is a sign that our brain is not running well.

When our children were infants, we would put them to sleep early in the evening. Later, before going to bed, I would tiptoe in to look at them as they slept. In the darkness of their room, my face would beam the light of joy as I watched them sleep. I could hardly contain my pleasure as I drank in how precious they were to me. If I imagine my heavenly Father doing that to me, I can feel joy in my stomach. I can feel my body react to my Father's face. The physical human body was designed to respond to joy.

Joy illustrates the importance of our bodies while walking with Jesus. We are meant to sense the emotional signals of life in our flesh and bones. God designed us to feel His presence, but in my experience this aspect of discipleship was missing. When was the last time your church offered a class on "feeling God in your body"? It might even sound creepy to our modern ears. Joy is a visceral response to our relationship with God. Remember the response when pregnant Mary visited her cousin: "When Elizabeth heard Mary's greeting, the baby leaped in her womb, and Elizabeth was filled with the Holy Spirit" (Luke 1:41). Our whole bodies respond as we encounter the living God.

The Benefits of Joy

As I studied more about the role of joy in spiritual formation, I saw the benefits piling up. When Jim told me that he discovered the importance of joy and brought it to his counseling practice, he saw drastic changes in the lives of his patients. His clinic treated difficult cases that other clinics and churches had given up on, and most patients arrived to their first session in a state of severely low joy. Previously, the clinic would need to hospitalize a large percentage of these patients during their treatment. Their counseling sessions would send them into such deep trauma that they could no longer function. Jim and the other therapists had come to accept that hospitalization was a normal part of recovery.

Once the clinic started focusing on building patients' joy before treating their trauma, hospitalization rates plummeted to almost zero. They were filling up their clients' gas tanks with joy fuel before beginning the heavy work of trauma recovery. Trying to do emotionally taxing work with an empty tank is like running a marathon without having eaten food for a month. Eventually your body will shut down for lack of energy. Jim's patients would emotionally collapse. We run the same danger in our churches and families when we do not build our joy together as a part of ministry. We eventually drain our tanks and run on empty.

Joy helps us regulate our emotions and endure suffering. Jesus refused to relinquish joy in the midst of His suffering on the cross. When we are able to stay relationally connected to others and God, we experience joy while we suffer. Joy does not remove our pain, but it gives us the strength to endure. Remember that joy is relational, so "joy in suffering" means that God and our community are glad to be with us in our distress. They do not allow us to suffer alone. We are able to bear our suffering like Jesus, "who for the joy set before Him endured the cross" (Heb. 12:2 NASB).

Contrary to what some preachers say in their sermons on Jesus' "seven last words," He never lost touch of His Father's face shining on Him as He was tortured and humiliated.[3] "For the joy set before him he endured the cross, scorning its shame, and sat down at the right hand of the throne of God" (Heb. 12:2). He could see through the angry faces in the crowd to the kind and steady gaze of His Father. His joy sustained Him. The author of Hebrews exhorts us to handle our suffering the same way, "fixing our eyes on Jesus, the author and perfecter of faith" (12:2 NASB). Jesus' face helps us persevere through the pain of life.

It is important to remember that joy is not strictly an emotion. We might refer to it as a supra-emotion because it can go on top of and connect with other emotions. For example, if I lose my job, this is usually not considered a joyful occasion. Instead, I am probably feeling some combination of sadness, fear, and anger. However, when I experience these unpleasant emotions and can simultaneously feel that God is with me, I have added joy into the mix. If I have close friends who are also happy to be with me in my loss, my joy magnifies even more. Now I'm feeling sad *and* joyful. Fearful *and* joyful. Angry *and* joyful. Joy does not replace the unpleasant emotions; instead it combines with my emotions to keep me relationally connected in distress.

The importance of joy to our brain highlights the fact that we must suffer in community. We were not meant to suffer alone. We need to lean on God and on our people in times of distress. We naturally do this when a family member dies. Everyone comes together in order to share the sadness. We tell stories about the deceased. We eat together. We sit in silence. We are joyful (not happy) because we want to suffer together. This is the definition of joy: I want to be with you. Joy is relational in its essence.

Joy is the foundation for a secure bond with God. When I trust that God is happy to be with me[4] and is smiling at me, this joy naturally removes fear from the relationship. A goal we have in our bond with God is to nurture a loving relationship until it has no fear. One of Jesus' disciples explains it well: "There is no fear in love. But perfect love drives out fear, because fear has to do with punishment. The one who fears is not made perfect in love" (1 John 4:18). Joy is the path to a fearless love for God.

Our identity is built and formed by joy-bonded relationships. The identity center in our brain grows in response to joy, which helps us act like ourselves in all situations. In a performance-based relationship or community, our identity becomes distorted because we feel the need to perform. When we put on a pretend self, our joy starts decreasing. We can build joy only with our true self. When churches foster a performance-based environment that encourages us to simply put on a happy face when we are suffering, it will quickly run out of joy. We will explore the importance of our identity in chapter 5.

I have already mentioned that joy helps us experience God's presence in our bodies. I could keep listing more benefits, but let me quote a book Jim coauthored:

> When we are the sparkle in someone's eyes, their face lights up with a smile when they see us. We feel joy. From the moment we are born, joy shapes the chemistry, structure and growth of our brain. Joy lays the foundation for how well we will handle relationships, emotions, pain and pleasure throughout our lifetime. Joy creates an identity that is stable and consistent over time. Joy gives us the freedom to share our hearts with God and others. Expressing our joyful identity creates space for others to belong. Joy gives us the freedom to live without masks because, in spite of our weaknesses, we know we are loved. We are not afraid of our vulnerabilities or exposure. Joy

gives us the freedom from fear to live from the heart Jesus gave us. We discover increasing delight in becoming the people God knew we could be.[5]

God designed us to live on a rich diet of joy-filled relationships. Communities that take joy building seriously will experience all of the benefits listed above and more. Since joy happens when people are glad to be together, take a moment to remember your own experiences in joyful groups. Have you seen any of these benefits of joy?

- I feel like I belong
- I feel more stable when things go wrong
- It is easier to be myself
- I feel free to share my heart with God and others

Increasing Joy Capacity

When I learned that joy was relational and often nonverbal, I asked Jim at one gathering, "How do I increase my joy?" He looked at me across the table and asked me to close my eyes. He said, "Think of a memory that makes you feel grateful and connected to God in that moment." Then he told me to go back and relive the experience for ten seconds. I closed my eyes and went back to a memory in the mountains of Colorado. I sensed God encouraging me as I watched a red-tailed hawk. I remembered seeing the wind ruffling the feathers of its neck as it sat on top of a ponderosa pine tree.

I opened my eyes as Jim asked me to give the memory a short title. I didn't hesitate. "Red-tailed hawk."

Jim then asked me what I felt in my body when I relived red-tailed hawk. I sat in silence for a few seconds. It was hard for me to describe. "It feels like a cramp of excitement between my chest and my stomach."

Next he asked, "What do you think God might have been wanting to impress on you by that memory?" I had to sit for a while. This was not natural for me, so I closed my eyes again, and as I remembered the wind ruffling the feathers of the hawk, I answered, "God is reminding me that He loves me and is with me, and I also sense that He is very glad I am in this room right now learning from you."

Jim said that this exercise is designed to increase a person's joy capacity. He instructed all of us around the table to start a list of grateful memories with the goal of having at least ten. "Red-tailed hawk is your first entry. Use the list to go into five minutes of nonverbal gratitude every day."

Nonverbal gratitude is right-brained. No words are necessary, just memories. I usually need to use several on my list to maintain a state of gratitude for five solid minutes. Jim stressed that it was important for each memory to have two characteristics: (1) I am aware of the sensations in my body as I relive it, and (2) I feel some sort of connection with God in the memory. These two characteristics assure that my right brain stays involved in the practice. Otherwise it can easily shift toward left-brained gratitude (words) instead of right brained gratitude (images, autobiographical memories, relational connection, body integration). Building joy is a right-brain dominant exercise.

In the book *Joyful Journey*, Jim and his coauthors explain the importance of gratitude: "When we keep practicing gratitude with God our brain remembers what our connection with Him was like making it easier for us to find our way back to Him."[6] Gratitude is the first step to building joy into our lives and helps us experience a more consistent attachment with God. We do not directly choose to be more joyful any more than we can choose to

When we keep practicing gratitude with God our brain remembers what our connection with Him was like making it easier for us to find our way back to Him.

have lower blood pressure. The joy and blood pressure systems in the brain are not subject to direct choice. Joy levels are regulated indirectly through relationships. Increasing joy will involve improving our relational skills, training our brain, and getting involved in tightly bonded community.

Filling a person with joy fuels their brain with relational energy. When our bodies can feel the glow of Jesus' face shining on us, our joy capacity grows. As our joy grows, our faces shine on each other, which makes other people feel joy. When we throw in some intentional practices to magnify joy, we are on the way to creating a high-joy community. We are adding an essential nutrient to replenish our spiritual soil.

Practice builds our joy capacity, providing relational energy to everything else. Our joy capacity can grow in size as we learn to fill ourselves with joy. The size of our joy tank grows. The first skills I was taught as a young Christian were to read Scripture and pray. These practices are important and helpful and have formed who I am, but I was not taught how to refill when my tank gets drained. I was never trained to experience joy in the middle of painful emotions.

As our tight-knit college group slowly dispersed, I felt my joy start to sink. The high-joy life I had taken for granted for eight years suddenly felt elusive. I knew little about joy at the time, so I described myself as "feeling a little off." I kept going to church, reading the Bible, and praying, but I was running on empty.

Feelings of hopelessness crept into my life, eventually bottoming out in depression. What was I doing wrong?

The Low-Joy Life

The human brain was designed to look for and run on joy. My joy drops when I sense few faces shining on me and few people happy to be with me. I may start believing that God is no longer happy to be with me. I am isolated and lonely. If my community is not in the habit of expressing what God sees as special in each of us, our eyes do not meet and our faces do not shine when we see each other. Our soil becomes depleted. When we do not understand how joy works, we miss the treasure before our eyes.

Since joy helps us regulate painful emotions, when it runs low, we will look to nonrelational sources to stop the pain. Soil that is low on joy is primed for growing addictions. When our brain looks for joy and does not find it, we become vulnerable to "pseudo-joys." These are substances and experiences that trick our brain to temporarily shut off the unpleasant emotions, but they are nonrelational and ultimately unsatisfying.

Joy substitutes can appear on the surface to be normal things, like food, social media, and shopping. The more obvious pseudo-joys are alcohol, drugs, sugar, and porn. Low-joy cultures will see an increase in these pseudo-joy addictions. Increasing our joy will naturally calm our cravings for pseudo-joys, and building joy should be an integrated part of any addiction program.

When we ignore the importance of joy in our churches, we leave an important variable to chance. When our joy is running low, much of life does not function. Imagine that you are on the support team for a Formula One race car. You are going through your prerace checklist right before a race. You diligently check the

THE OTHER HALF OF CHURCH

oil, tires, and fluids, but an important item is not on your checklist. There is no line item to ensure the gas tank is filled. If you skip checking the gas tank, your car may work well or not. It depends on whether someone remembered to fill the tank.

As a pastor, this analogy explains a mistake I made. I led discipleship trainings that did not take joy into account. What I saw was inconsistency. I was left scratching my head, wondering what was going wrong. The training worked well for some people and not for others. This made sense when I learned the function of joy. If half of the people arrive to my training with their tanks already full, and the other half arrive on empty, what would you expect? I had failed to make sure everyone was fueled up for the training. Now I would use the measures and exercises like those in the "Try It Out" section at the end of this chapter.

Joy Leaks

Churches and families often have reasons why their joy is low. We call these "joy leaks," and we must find where joy is leaking and plug the holes. One cause of draining joy is a lack of development around the six big emotions (sadness, anger, fear, shame, disgust, and despair). Creating a path from the big emotions to joy allows our brain to regulate the emotions instead of getting stuck in them. Regulation means that we stay relationally connected and continue to be the person God created us to be when we suffer.

This concept of creating paths to joy might be new to you, so I will explain. When I experience a big distressing emotion that has not been connected to joy, my personality will change, and I will tend to isolate. These undeveloped emotional paths cause joy levels to drop because I get stuck and isolated in the unpleasant emotion. When I am stuck, I lose my true identity and start acting like a different person. We all have experienced this breakdown of our identity and have seen it in others. I once had a boss who liked me and treated me well. When he became angry, however, he acted like a crazy person. He was cruel, abrupt, and distant. He stopped acting like himself.

One of the joy-building exercises is designed to build a path from all of the difficult emotions to joy. This pathway allows me to suffer and remain joyful. Not happy, but joyful. My people and my God pull me through because they are glad to be with me in my suffering.[7]

Building resilience in difficult emotions is like buying a new cabin on a lake that has no path down to the dock. The first few trips to the dock take time and effort with a shovel and a machete. Following the path gets easier until, after a hundred trips, you have a well-worn path between the cabin and the dock. My wife and I are currently training to connect the big six emotions to joy. In the training we start treading the path between difficult emotions and joy. Repetition is needed to build the path, but the results are visceral. My wife and I can feel that our inner emotional structure is changing. We are able to remain joyful in distressing emotions that would have previously left us feeling isolated.[8]

Since starting this training, I often have encounters with strong emotions that I can now regulate. I recently went fishing with friends on the Eagle River outside of Vail, Colorado. The Eagle River is known for its difficult wading. It is full of large boulders that one fly shop owner called "snot covered bowling balls." I could attest to the accuracy of his vivid description when I snagged my fly on a log in the middle of the river. I needed to wade across to unhook my fly, so I took my time and carefully placed each step. I was able to retrieve my flies.

As I made my way back, I took a step and slipped on one

bowling ball and then another until I lost my footing completely and went under. I smashed my knee on a boulder and almost filled my waders with freezing water. As I awkwardly dog paddled and then picked myself up, I felt the adrenaline surging through my body and the familiar emotional wave coming. I had done this before. Then my training kicked in. I took a few deep breaths, quieted myself, and started talking to Jesus. Within a minute, I was able to laugh about it. Two years previous, before my training, I would have sunk into a stew of anger and shame that would have lasted twenty minutes. Here I was, back on my feet and laughing in a minute! No joy leaked that day.

Another culprit that leaks joy is unresolved trauma. From the brain's perspective, trauma happens anytime we suffer alone. Suffering turns into trauma when we are unable to process our suffering with God and other people. Trauma is stored in our brain, in circuits of flesh, kind of like an armed mousetrap. When something goes wrong that feels like a previous trauma to our brain, not only do we experience unpleasant emotions, but our trauma gets triggered. The mousetrap goes *SNAP!* The trauma magnifies the already big feelings, and we get stuck in distress.

After we recover, we will often wonder, *Why did I overreact so much?* We may have no conscious memory of the trauma, but our right brain remembers. When we see an emotional reaction that is disproportionate to the circumstances, we are likely seeing the stored energy of unhealed trauma. Healing these stored emotions is beyond the scope of this book, but you will not be surprised to learn that it requires a full-brained treatment. When you heal trauma, the energy stored in the traumatic memory dissipates and is no longer triggerable. You have just plugged a hole in your joy tank! See Further Resources for This Chapter for more information on healing trauma.

Another joy leak is the prevalence of video screens in our

daily lives. We use smartphones, television, and movie screens to fill our idle minutes or hours. Joy and screen time are inversely proportional.[9] When our eyes and face are staring at our phones, we are not engaging with the faces around us. The joy drains out of our communities by depriving ourselves of each other's faces. Our need for face-to-face time is designed into our flesh and cannot be substituted with a screen. Our brains can distinguish between a real face and a face on a screen even when we are infants. Our neurological circuits do not react to screens the same as they do to live faces. Since we need facial joy like we need food and oxygen, we are starving ourselves of relational nutrition. Parents can start by putting limits on screen time and emphasizing face-to-face conversation. You will be surprised how different you and your family will feel when you look at each other in the face. Plugging this joy leak will involve being countercultural. Churches must lead the way by restoring joy to our soil.

Finally, a narcissist in the community rips a gaping hole in our joy tank. A church or family will have a hard time raising joy without patching this hole, and it is a difficult hole to repair. The goal of this book is to explain how we create spiritual soil that grows character and is resistant to the growth of narcissism. A narcissistic person has a hard time thriving and growing roots in healthy soil. As the saying goes, "An ounce of prevention is worth a pound of cure." Handling a narcissist who is already rooted in your community, possibly as a leader, is beyond the scope of this book. Jim Wilder has written at length on this topic in *The Pandora Problem*. (See Further Resources for This Chapter.) The teaching and training in *The Pandora Problem* are designed to help heal narcissism that is already in the church. Maintaining joy and acting like ourselves in the presence of narcissism is advanced discipleship requiring well-developed maturity.

Increasing Joy in Your Community

After hearing Jim explain the importance of joy and understanding how God designed our brains for joy, I wondered how to fit this into my job as a pastor of spiritual formation. For four years, I had been designing a step-by-step path to maturity for the members of our church. It included learning theology, reading Scripture, and practicing spiritual disciplines. I wondered where joy would fit into my current plan, and it became obvious that joy is the first step. Since nothing else works well when joy is low, it makes sense to fill up the gas tank at the beginning.

If we desire to fulfill the Great Commission, we will turn our churches into high-joy environments. This is a community where our faces light up when we see each other. We practice helping each other increase joy capacity as part of our regular practices. Our community is contagious when people come and see our joyful interactions. Young or old, Christian or not, our brains hunger for joy.

In the first years of life our joy comes from our caretakers. Later, as adults, we can intentionally increase our joy capacity, and this work will improve our brain chemistry. Many low-joy friendships can quickly be energized simply by learning about joy and taking action to build capacity. Since my wife and I learned about the importance of joy, we are intentional about slowing down and letting our faces shine on each other. I let my wife know, using my face and eyes, how special she is to me. If I've had a hard day and my joy is low, I will take Claudia's hand and we will sit on the couch facing each other. We let our eyes meet and smile as we enjoy our connection. We don't stare but settle into a nice rhythm of using our faces to nonverbally communicate, "I am glad to be with you." We do this for several seconds and then close our eyes and breathe deeply. Then we reengage. Occasionaly we talk, but words are not necessary. We do this exercise, in rhythm, for several minutes, and I quickly feel my joy rising.

Just like Claudia and I had to change our patterns in order to build more joy, turning our churches into high-joy environments will require changes. Church styles may be entrenched, so these changes may not come easily. Improving each soil nutrient will present new challenges that we will address as we go. Remember that joy is a right-brain dominant emotion requiring face-to-face interactions. We need to learn to embrace eye contact. Churches are often configured to support left-brain dominant activities: thinking, doctrine, words, and strategies. The first challenge might be arranging our meetings in a way that promotes eye contact. Current formats offer little time or intention to focus on relational joy. In fact, some people hate the idea of having to stop and interact during church. It does not seem like what we should do in church.

Making changes to create joy will be uncomfortable for some. The other half of church will touch areas of our lives that are unfamiliar. Leaders and worshipers might hear complaints about changing what is comfortable. Someone may protest that the church is growing in size and giving. "Why upset things by trying to increase joy?" Character formation and building joy are inextricably linked. Jesus prayed for the joyful character of His followers when

> **Only when we are convinced that character transformation is the central task of the church will we be intentional about raising the level of joy.**

He prayed that they may have "the full measure of my joy within them" (John 17:13). Only when we are convinced that character transformation is the central task of the church will we be intentional about raising joy. Leaders and worshipers must both be involved in making these changes.

The first step for increasing joy is establishing effective gratitude practices. One friend of mine likes to say, "Gratitude is the on-ramp to joy." You read above how Jim introduced me to a gratitude exercise. The thirty-day Joy on Demand exercise (Appendix B) is an easy practice to introduce to your community. When we all start practicing gratitude each day and sharing our experiences in our gatherings, we are ramping up joy together. See Appendix B for a fuller explanation of this exercise.

Another practice for increasing joy may be uncomfortable for many Western people and may even seem risky. If joy is transmitted primarily through our faces and eyes, we need to practice letting our faces light up with each other. There is some danger to this practice, so we must handle it wisely. We require that, unless you are a married couple or family members, facial joy exercises should be done in groups of three, not two. The hormones released as we build joy can easily be confused for romantic feelings, and this can lead to emotional misunderstanding and inappropriate interactions. Training is not meant to be a matchmaking opportunity, and this confusion can destabilize the entire community.

Married couples will benefit greatly from building joy together. Just last night, my wife and I built our joy by looking into each other's eyes and delighting in each other. We practice building facial joy together for five minutes several times a week.[10] We do not engage in a staring contest; instead we build joy for ten seconds and then we both close our eyes for several seconds. We cycle between building joy and disconnecting briefly, then building joy again. This cycle of joy-quiet-joy-quiet is the same cycle that God designed to energize the formation of a baby's brain, and it works for adults, too. Building joy involves a cycle of joy and then disconnecting to quiet ourselves.[11]

In church training, we perform this same exercise in groups of three. In this case, you can practice with complete strangers and build joy together. It helps to be guided the first time by someone who has experience building joy in this joy-quiet cycle. Since this practice is new to most people, training needs to be accompanied by good teaching offering the biblical basis for building joy. Further Resources for This Chapter contains explanation and practices designed to build joy.

In small groups, something as simple as greeting each person with a brief eye-to-eye connection and telling them how happy you are to see them raises the joy in your group. Small groups also would benefit by incorporating intentional practices of joy and gratitude. Start your group by having each person share a gratitude story from their week. We also increase joy by telling each other what we find special in them.

Raising the joy level in a family starts with the parents. As with most of the right-brain work we do, I cannot pass a skill to my child through words alone. I must practice the skill myself. To raise joy in a family, the first step is to raise the joy of the parents. You and your spouse can enjoy the benefits of doing the Thirty-day Joy on Demand exercise in Appendix B. The joy you build will quickly spill over into the entire family.

Families benefit when the parents intentionally build joy with each other and their children. Parents can make changes to their family structure to balance screen-centered family time with face-centered times. Looking our children in the face and telling them how special they are sets them up for a life full of relational energy. During dinner time, Claudia and I sometimes go around the table and share something for which we are grateful. Even when our children are having problems with behavior or school, we can still be happy to be with them. God is also happy to be with us, even when our lives are a mess. A beautiful trait of joy is that it does not require good circumstances. Another step we take to build joy in our family is to make our dining table a phone-free zone. All eyes are up and looking at each other as we enjoy a meal.

- -

When we church leaders fail to build joy among our people, we allow people to run their lives with their spiritual gas tanks on empty. Our people are deprived of an essential relational nutrient for a healthy soil that supports discipleship. When we discover ways to build joy together, we awaken the relational half of church that our busy culture squeezes out of our lives. Joy puts us on the path to transformation.

- -

GROUP DISCUSSION QUESTIONS

Read several of the following Scriptures on joy: Numbers 6:25; Psalms 4:6–7; 31:16; 44:3; 67:1; 80:3, 7, 19; Daniel 9:17.

1. Pick a few of the Scriptures above and read them together. How does that feel in your body as you hear of God's face shining on you?
2. Read Psalm 4:6–7. Why might David value the light of the Lord's face shining on him more than financial security (abundant grain and wine)?
3. Rephrase the joy Scriptures below and replace "joy" with the concept of God's face shining on you. He is happy to be

with you. Read them to each other.

    a. James 1:2: *"Consider it pure joy, my brothers and sisters, whenever you face trials of many kinds."*

    b. Romans 15:13: *"May the God of hope fill you with all joy and peace as you trust in him, so that you may overflow with hope by the power of the Holy Spirit."*

TRY IT OUT

1. Take the *Soil Sample 1: Relational Joy Level* evaluation in Appendix A. Discuss the results in your group.
2. Fill out the pseudo-joy checklist in Appendix C. Share what pseudo joys are most attractive to you when your relational joy runs low.
3. In your group, select a volunteer, and have the others share something they are grateful for in that person. Go around the circle repeating this for each person. This exercise builds joy in your group.
4. As a group, start the thirty-day Gratitude exercise and share your progress during the month. See Appendix B for a fuller explanation of this exercise.

FURTHER RESOURCES FOR THIS CHAPTER

Explanation of Jesus' last words:

- Refer to JIMTalks, Volume 13, "07_13_Singing," https://shop. lifemodelworks.org/collections/jimtalks-munchies/products/munchies-volume-14

Relational and emotional brain skills:

- See thrivetoday.org/thrive

Building joy:

- Chris M. Coursey, *Transforming Fellowship: 19 Brain Skills That Build Joyful Community*; for information on joy theory and practice and the joy-quiet cycle, read chapters 3–6.
- Wilder, Khouri, Coursey, Sutton, *Joy Starts Here: The Transformation Zone*

Healing trauma:

- Wilder, Kang, Loppnow, Loppnow, *Joyful Journey: Listening to Immanuel*
- The extensive writings and videos of Karl D. Lehman, MD, at KCLehman.com; this material is more technical than that in *Joyful Journey*
- Chris Coursey and E. James Wilder, *Share Immanuel: The Healing Lifestyle*

Narcissism:

- E. James Wilder, *The Pandora Problem*

4

. . . .

Hesed:
Our Relational Glue

"Anyone who loves me will obey my teaching. . . .
Anyone who does not love me will not obey my teaching."

John 14:23–24

May the Lord make you increase and abound in love
for one another and for all, as we do for you.

1 Thessalonians 3:12 ESV

AS I GOT INVOLVED in my Christian community at college, I started seeing spontaneous changes in my life. I could feel a bond forming among us all. We loved being together and felt Jesus in our midst. Our group invented reasons to gather. I received daily affirmations. They were glad I was part of their lives. We were becoming a family. I saw my values change, not because I tried to change them, but because I seemed to absorb a new perspective from my community. My life changed, not because of my own intention, but because of love.

My prior experience of community centered around shared interests—humor, partying, skiing, running, and playing jazz. People who shared my sense of humor tended to become my friends. Dorm residents who partied and went skiing with me entered my circle of companions. Playing jazz until the late hours of the night also created a community of common enjoyment. We bonded as we improvised.

My new community was different. The glue holding us together was not primarily shared interests but shared love. Our love was spontaneous. We were in the habit of eating together in the dorm cafeteria. One night, Karen sat down at our table with tears in her eyes. She had come straight from a lecture and shared how the professor had humiliated her in front of the class. On the walk back to our hall, a friend and I wondered how we could encourage her. We grabbed two guitars in my room and ran over to Karen's hall. Under her third floor window, we started throwing pebbles at the glass to get her attention. As soon as she opened the window, we started serenading her, singing, "I'm in the Mood for Love." Others opened their windows and enjoyed our harmonies, and when we finished, we received applause from a sizeable audience. The next day, Karen told us, "You have no idea how much that helped me." Spontaneous acts of love were commonplace in our spiritual family.

Over thirty years later, a large group of us reunited to celebrate the family we had experienced in the university. We caught up and shared story after story. We all sang an old hymn that we had sung every week in college. Many of us hadn't sung this song for thirty years. Our eyes blurred with tears of joy as we sang. We were glad to be together.

Attachment

After meeting with Jim a few times, my wife and I were so excited about what we were learning that we gathered a group of friends and introduced them to Jim and his wife, Kitty. We began meeting every week to put our new knowledge into practice—something I hope you will do as well.

In our gatherings with Jim and Kitty, I expected to hear about the brain and joy. Instead, Jim talked about *hesed*. Jim used the Hebrew word *hesed* to describe what neuroscientists call attachment. I had never heard *hesed* described as relational attachment. Over and over, he emphasized the importance of our attachments to each other. Attachment is an essential soil nutrient for forming our character the way my first community molded me.

Like my first crop of tomatoes, this experience of Christian community was abundantly fruitful. Our relational soil was rich in *hesed*, the second ingredient of healthy soil. I intentionally placed this strange word in the chapter title because it expresses what we often know but cannot put in words. *Hesed* describes something we find in the brain and in the Bible.

Our brains draw life from our strongest relational attachments to grow our character and develop our identity. Who we love shapes who we are. Character formation is the central task of the church. Our brains are designed to use our attachments to form our character. We should expect to find the concept of attachment all over Scripture. Attachments are so indispensable to brain development that Jim set out to find them in the Bible. He found what he was seeking in the Hebrew word *hesed*.

I learned in seminary that *hesed* was an "enduring covenant love," but I did not think of enduring love as an attachment. You have unknowingly bumped into the word *hesed* if you have read the Old Testament. Hebrew scholars admit that it is difficult to

Our brains draw life from our strongest relational attachments to grow our character and develop our identity. Who we love shapes who we are.

capture the nuances of *hesed* with a single word in English, so translators often use several words in modern languages. Lamentations 3:22 is a useful example: *"The steadfast love of the Lord never ceases."* *Hesed* here, in the English Standard Version, is translated "steadfast love." In different versions of the Bible, *hesed* is translated "great love" (NIV), "loyal kindness" (NET), "lovingkindness" (NASB), "mercies" (KJV), "faithful love" (NLT).

Hesed is forever in search of a translation into other languages because of its wide range of meaning. This Hebrew word carries the sense of an enduring connection that brings life and all good things into a relationship. *Hesed* is a kind and loyal care for the well-being of another. Jim and his friend Dr. Marcus Warner, a former Hebrew professor, found *hesed* as they were searching for the concept of attachment in the Bible. They were convinced that the most powerful force in the human brain surely would show itself in Scripture. The central characteristic of becoming human through a loving and enduring attachment must be somewhere in the language of both the Old and New Testaments. Hebrew offered only one good candidate and one that could be found all over the text, and it was *hesed*.[1]

Greek likewise has a word for the love that attaches all Christians to God and to one another, and that is *agape*, a very obscure Greek word until Christians started using it. However, Saint Paul found *agape* inadequate to convey what he meant and took all of

1 Corinthians 13 to fill in the meaning he sought to communicate. It was as though he were trying to expand *agape* to include what came naturally with *hesed*.[2]

New Testament authors find it necessary to add adjectives and elaborations to enhance the meaning of *agape*. Peter does this in his first letter where he writes, "Love one another deeply, from the heart" (1 Peter 1:22). Later in this same letter, he writes, "Above all, love each other deeply, because love covers over a multitude of sins" (4:8). Paul similarly enhances *agape* with the image of a beloved child: "Follow God's example, therefore, as dearly loved children and walk in the way of love, just as Christ loved us" (Eph. 5:1–2).

As I heard about the importance of attachment, I wondered, *Did* hesed *describe the relational glue that held my first spiritual family together in college?* A high-*hesed* community is bound together by strong and lasting attachments. Ideally, spouses, family, and close friends naturally enjoy *hesed* relationships. Was *hesed* what glued me and Jesus together? Did He want our love (our attachment) to change me? Could this be what held Claudia and me together? I heard my children laughing together, and I wondered, *Is* hesed *how I love them?* As I looked around at the people in our group, I hoped this relational glue would form us into a family.

I asked Jim to elaborate on his understanding of *hesed*, and this time he talked about the brain. Attachment is the strongest force in the human brain.[3] It is not an emotion, although we feel it strongly, and attachment runs much deeper in the brain below willful control. Attachment is the best word scientists could find for what glues people together and little creatures to their parents. It produces an enduring care for the well-being of another. Attachment is a life-giving forever bond with no mechanism in the brain to unglue us. If God has an enduring love for us that brings us good, the only force in the human brain that can understand such lasting kindness and care is the brain's attachment system.

Jim used the analogy of contact cement. He once had a job mounting panels on a wall using contact cement. He painted the panels and the wall with the glue, and then carefully pressed the two together. Once they touched, there was no going back. If he flinched at the last minute and pressed one on crookedly, it would be crooked forever. He would have to destroy the wall and the panel to pull it off. This may seem like an unusual analogy for love, but *hesed* attachment has real sticking power. Without strong relational attachments, our soil remains depleted of a nutrient that is essential for growing character.

The love described by *hesed* and *agape* is deep and dear, requiring more than a single word. In English, the word *love* is used in so many ways that it has lost its weight. When we come across love in the Bible, we often fail to grasp the profound meaning because the word has been worn out with overuse in our culture. We use the word *hesed* in an attempt to freshen and restore the depth of meaning. It is a Hebrew word that we believe should become familiar to all Christians.

Hesed and the Brain

Perhaps the biggest surprise emerging from brain-scan studies has been that, for our brain, identity develops through attachments. Joyful, secure attachments build a good brain. Fearful or weak attachments build a bad brain. When we say "a bad brain," we mean an identity center that damages our relationships when we are upset. Character develops through relationships—*hesed* relationships[4]—that can handle times when things go wrong. A secure *hesed* attachment can ride through storms and remain loving. Character in the brain is an expression of an identity that has grown strong and well. As Christians, we want an identity in our brain that looks like Jesus.

Jim describes how identity forms our brain: "Our primary identity, and the apex of the neurological control structure of the brain, *is a relational one*"[5] (emphasis mine). The prefrontal cortex grows to become about one sixth of the brain and is configured with neurological circuits representing three faces engaged with each other. Infant brains develop identity through joyful interactions usually with the mother and the father. The joyful faces of the parents are combined with the baby's growing sense of self to form a triad of joyful interaction. In this ideal environment, joy becomes the baby's strength, and this lays a foundation for a lifelong joyful identity.

There is a lot to unpack in that paragraph. When Claudia and I first heard about the brain's identity center, we were blown away. We had visited the Wilders one afternoon when he explained the three faces of our prefrontal cortex. These three viewpoints form one single identity as they work together. My wife exclaimed, "Three faces sounds familiar. Did God design our brains based on the pattern of the Trinity?" We were not sure whether theologians would agree, but it made us wonder.

If God's attachments are *hesed*, what happens when a baby does not have this joyful triangle? If the parents' faces are fearful during this stage of the baby's growth, or if the parents are detached, the baby's identity does not develop from a foundation of joy and love. In this relational soil, the identity of the infant becomes unstable and disorganized. Jim adds, "Isn't it like God to design a brain that only knows itself in relationship, and then only when that relationship is one of love?"[6]

A similar dynamic happens in the church. Jesus intends His church to function as a family that is bonded together with joyful attachments of love. Like a baby with her two smiling parents, our churches can create environments for developing our joyful identities as children of God. When we live in a family of joyful *hesed* relationships, we put our brains into the ideal zone for developing us into the image of Christ. We are filled with joy and surrounded with stable, deep attachments. Our prefrontal cortex is energized to build a stable identity.

When our churches or communities have fear-based attachments to each other and to God, this creates a chaotic environment for growth.[7] If attachments are weak or transitory instead of secure, development will be stunted. The neurological circuits that Jesus designed to build us into His image are running on empty. The soil is depleted.

When my initial Christian community dispersed and I got involved in other groups and churches, I often sensed that something was missing. I thought, *This does not feel like my first Christian community. Why?* Over the following thirty years, I have found weak *hesed* to be the rule instead of the exception. I had difficulty developing the deep bonds that I had before, and I did not know what to do. I thought, *Why aren't all Christian communities deeply loving?*

Jim and others believe that an Enlightenment model of transformation has influenced our churches, and this is why joy and love are no longer the central characteristics of Christian discipleship.[8] According to Enlightenment thinking the formula for transformation is:

$$\text{transformation} = \text{truth} + \text{good choices} + \text{power.}[9]$$

It is easy to believe that if our Christian communities have solid biblical teaching and doctrine (truth) and we are encouraged to apply the teaching to our lives (good choices), the Holy Spirit will enable us to understand the truth and make good choices (power). We expect this will lead to transformation. The formula looks reasonable to modern eyes, but it has a fatal flaw—it is missing the most important variable. Love, the primary mover of character, is absent. Without *hesed*, we see little transformation.

I will carefully remind you, we are not suggesting that truth, choices, and power have no place in discipleship. We are restoring *hesed* to its central place. In their book, *The Solution of Choice*, Jim Wilder and Marcus Warner explain the role of love in discipleship:

> When hesed replaces truth as the foundation of discipleship, the whole model self-corrects. Placing love at the core of the transformation process allows truth, choice, and power to play their proper roles and not bear a weight they were never intended to carry. . . . *Developments in modern brain science have made it clear that any model of transformation and character change must be anchored in the development of a love bond with God and His people.*[10] (italics mine)

Once I understood the importance of attachment in forming character, I began to see examples all over Scripture. For example, Jesus emphasizes the role of attachment (*agapao*) in discipleship in John 14:23, "Anyone who loves me will obey my teaching." Just to make sure the disciples understood, Jesus repeated it again using negative logic. "Anyone who does not love me will not obey my teaching" (John 14:24). Our attachment to Jesus produces obedience. In order to fulfill the Great Commission, both Scripture and brain science emphasize that we must start by building joyful *hesed* attachments. We must convert to a new model of discipleship, a *hesed* model, where relationships are in the center of everything.

The Centrality of *Hesed* in Scripture

You will see a pattern in this book. Recent findings in neuroscience are strongly supported in Scripture. We get this in spades with *hesed*. Not only is love mentioned often in the New Testament (348 times), *agape/hesed* is the dominant feature of a community living in God's kingdom. Jesus came to establish a *hesed* community on earth. This starts when God forms a *hesed* bond with us in Christ. John writes, "See what great love the Father has lavished on us, that we should be called children of God! And that is what we are!" (1 John 3:1). God desires to lavish His love on His children. We are a spiritual family glued together by our Father's love.

If the central task of the church is to create a community of transformed disciples, we would expect Jesus' teaching to emphasize the centrality of love. We find that His words align with how He designed the circuitry in our brains. Let's look at a few examples.

A teacher of the law tested Jesus with a question:

"Teacher, which is the greatest commandment in the Law?"

Jesus replied: "'Love the Lord your God with all your heart and with all your soul and with all your mind.' This is the first and greatest commandment. And the second is like it: 'Love your neighbor as yourself.' All the Law and the Prophets hang on these two commandments" (Matt. 22:36–40).

The question was a trap, but Jesus sees it as an opportunity. In the eyes of heaven, love is the first and greatest force for living right and experiencing God's life on earth. According to Jesus, the rest of the numerous commands are specific examples of how we love God and each other. The concept of loving attachment flows through each command in the Old Testament law.

In John 15, Jesus uses the analogy of a branch and vine to explain our relationship to Him and the Father:

> "I am the vine; you are the branches. If you remain in me and I in you, you will bear much fruit; apart from me you can do nothing. . . . As the Father has loved me, so have I loved you. Now remain in my love. . . . My command is this: Love each other as I have loved you." (vv. 5, 9, 12)

The image of a vine and branch is a clear picture of attachment. We have an attachment to Jesus that bears fruit in our lives (character change). He presents a simple formula: no attachment, no fruit. Through the Father's attachment to Jesus, divine love flows to us through our connection to the vine. Our attachment to Jesus does not dead-end. The flow of divine sap courses through our attachments to each other. We see the stream of God's love spreading spiritual nutrition through our *hesed* attachments, from top to bottom. Our character is transformed through this flow of love. A *hesed* community has the Father's love in its veins and is bursting with fruit.

Think about the image of Jesus and you being a vine and a branch. Meditate on the closeness. Our *hesed* with Jesus is an attachment flowing with life, a strong and permanent bond. Jesus is attached to His Father, and He wants the same with us. He commands us to have the same attachment with each other. Jesus paints the picture of a *hesed* saturated network of attachments from our Father through Jesus into each other.

From their writings, we see that Jesus' disciples also understood the importance of love. John remembered well what Jesus taught him (in John 15) and elaborates in 1 John 4:

> Dear friends, let us love one another, for love comes from God. Everyone who loves has been born of God and knows God. Whoever does not love does not know God, because God is love. This is how God showed his love among us: He sent his one and only Son into the world that we might live through him. . . . Dear friends, since God so loved us, we also ought to love one another. No one has ever seen God; but if we love one another, God lives in us and his love is made complete in us. (vv. 7–9, 11–12)

Again we see the flow of love from God through His Son to us and through our attachments to each other. Our loving attachments to our Father, Jesus, and each other give us the clearest experience of the unseen God. Chapter 4 of John's first letter is his reminder that our Christian life is founded on *hesed/agape*. Without love, the Christian life collapses and ceases to be Christian. John adds later in chapter 4, "God is love. Whoever lives in love lives in God, and God in them" (v. 16). Love is our shining light to the world that God lives in us.

Paul wonders at the strength of our attachment to Jesus: "Who shall separate us from the love of Christ?" Is anyone or anything strong enough to break the relational glue that binds us to Jesus? Paul lists every possible culprit and arrives at the answer: Nobody! Nothing! "For I am convinced that neither death nor life, neither angels nor demons, neither the present nor the future, nor any powers, neither height nor depth, nor anything else in all creation, will be able to separate us from the love of God that is in Christ Jesus our Lord" (Rom. 8:38–39). Our *hesed* with Jesus is glue with a binding strength that nothing in all creation can break.

Hesed is not simply strong; *hesed* is also sweet. For Jesus, *hesed* attachments are family bonds. "Anyone who loves me will obey my teaching. My Father will love them, and we will come to them and make our home with them" (John 14:23). A *hesed* attachment produces a change in family structure. Jesus and His Father come to our home and knock on the door with their suitcases in hand. They move in and we become a family.

Jesus prays for another change of residence in the future: "Father, I want those you have given me to be with me where I am, and to see my glory" (John 17:24). Jesus also wants us to pack our bags and move in with Him someday. Until that happens, He is preparing rooms for His family members: "And if I go and prepare a place for you, I will come back and take you to be with me that you also may be where I am" (John 14:3).

Paul expounds on the familial nature of our bond with God in Romans 8:15–16: "The Spirit you received does not make you slaves, so that you live in fear again; rather, the Spirit you received brought about your adoption to sonship. And by him we cry, 'Abba, Father.' The Spirit himself testifies with our spirit that we are God's children." Our *hesed* attachment with God converts us from fearful slaves to delighted children.

In relationships of fear, our right brain can enter into a state similar to a muscle cramp, and the prefrontal cortex no longer allows transformation. God's *hesed* puts our prefrontal cortex back in the brain's working range by converting our fear into love and adopting us as His children.

We do not have to wait until we die to experience our heavenly family. Jesus desires His church to operate as a family here on earth. When He was teaching a crowd of people, someone informed Him that His mother and brothers had come and wanted to speak with Him. He replied, "Who is my mother, and who are my brothers?" Pointing to his disciples, he said, "Here are my mother and my brothers. For whoever does the will of my Father in heaven is my brother and sister and mother" (Matt. 12:48–50). Jesus is inaugurating a heavenly family of brothers and sisters who are attached to Him and each other.

As a young man, Peter heard Jesus speak these words. Many years later, as an old man, he addressed dispersed Christians as a "family of believers" (1 Peter 2:17; 5:9). He understood that we are the family of God, bound together as brothers and sisters, parents and children. The author of Hebrews agrees: "Both the one who makes people holy and those who are made holy are of the same family. So Jesus is not ashamed to call them brothers and sisters" (2:11). *Hesed* is the glue that binds us together as members of Jesus' family.

Most Christians know these verses on love, but the word itself has been drained of much of its meaning. When we read the word *love*, it does not land with the glory of its true substance. We would agree that we have a heavenly Father who loves us and that we are members of His family. If we fail to grasp the essence of love, these words blow by us like leaves in the wind.

A helpful exercise to revive this tired word is to replace "love" with the concept of attachment as we read these familiar Scriptures. For example, we looked at 1 John 4:11: "Dear friends, since God so loved us, we also ought to love one another." We can awaken our senses by replacing love with the idea of a family bond. A paraphrase might be, "Dear friends, since God has joyfully attached himself so firmly to us, we also ought to attach ourselves to each other as family members." You will awaken and broaden your definition of love in the Bible by doing this exercise as a part of your spiritual practices.

When we have an unclear understanding of love, our view of the church becomes distorted. We fail to see our fellowship in light of attachment. We may quote the Scriptures on love, but many of us do not love and live as a family. Even worse, many churches are intentionally configured in ways that keep *hesed* from growing.

Low-*Hesed* Christianity

As I look back on the early transformative years of my Christian life, I was growing in good soil. Our community was rich in joy and *hesed*. We were a spiritual family. I assumed most Christian communities were like mine. I was to learn otherwise.

As our full-brained spiritual community started to disperse, I gradually and unknowingly drifted toward a more left-brained spirituality. The relationships with friends in my first community were like family relationships. I knew many of them better and was more deeply attached to them than to my own parents and siblings. The level of attachment to people in many of my subsequent Christian communities was much weaker. The by-product for me was disappointing character formation. I was trying to grow fruit in depleted soil.

In subsequent Christian communities, I found that, with a few exceptions, *hesed* was *not* a priority. I met many people who had never experienced a *hesed* community in their lives. The inclination toward left-brained thinking had created weakly attached churches.

If the church follows the trends in our culture, weak attachments become normal. Creating a spiritual family is not a value or necessity. Unless Christians are willing to go against this cultural current, our soil will remain depleted. When we do not create a spiritual family with strong attachments, we cut off the flow of transformational power.

Low-*hesed* churches may look fine on the outside. People may be friendly and enthusiastic about their church. They might be excited about their five-year plans and bold strategies to grow and do great things. Prioritizing plans and vision above *hesed* attachments (the prime movers of growth) produces little transformation. Many churches do good things in their communities and around the world, but operate more like an efficiently run religious institution than a family. They do many good things but may not possess good character.

The Ephesian church is a prime example of a Christian community that started functioning like an institution instead of a family. Jesus offers his opinion of the Ephesian church in Revelation 2.

> I know your deeds, your hard work and your perseverance. I know that you cannot tolerate wicked people, that you have tested those who claim to be apostles but are not, and have found them false. You have persevered and have endured hardships for my name, and have not grown weary. (vv. 2–3)

This sounds pretty good so far. The Ephesian church is hardworking, and they don't give up. They have good doctrine and aren't corrupted by evil people who spread false teaching. They suffer for Jesus in a hostile city. If this were my church, I would be feeling optimistic so far, but Jesus is not finished:

> Yet I hold this against you: You have forsaken the love you had at first. Consider how far you have fallen! Repent and do the things you did at first. If you do not repent, I will come to you and remove your lampstand from its place. (vv. 4–5)

Ouch! It looked like they were doing everything well, but Jesus delivers a blunt rebuke. They stopped acting like a family and started functioning like an institution. We hear Jesus' opinion of a church that does many good things but does not function as a *hesed*-connected family. The consequence, if they do not restore their *hesed*, is that He will come and turn off the lights.

In the Sermon on the Mount, Jesus taught that the church should display the light of God to the world, and we should put that light on a lampstand so everyone can see (Matt. 5:14–16). However, in this case Jesus threatens the opposite. He will remove the lampstand of the Ephesian church because He does not want the church to shine. He wants them hidden under a bowl. A church without *hesed* no longer shines the light of Jesus, no matter how much ministry it may be doing. It may have perfect doctrine but, as one commentator writes, "Without love the congregation ceases to be a church."[11]

You might protest by saying that Jesus is talking about the church's love for Him and not their love for each other. It is instructive to notice that Jesus does not mention the object of their lost love. If we remember 1 John 4 that we studied above, John describes love as an intertwined attachment of the Father, the Son, and all of us. You cannot separate the loves. John elaborates on this:

Whoever claims to love God yet hates a brother or sister is a liar. For whoever does not love their brother and sister, whom they have seen, cannot love God, whom they have not seen. (1 John 4:20)

This is how we know that we love the children of God: by loving God and carrying out his commands. (1 John 5:2)

If we forsake our love for each other, we are also abandoning our love for Jesus. You cannot separate the two loves. We show our love for God by loving each other, and we demonstrate that we love each other by loving God. *Hesed* for God and each other is forever intertwined and cannot be separated. This is why I believe Jesus adds no object when He says that the Ephesian church lost their love. He was talking about our intermingled and inseparable love for Him, our Father, and each other. The Ephesian church stopped acting like a *hesed* family of loving attachments to each other and God.

In 1 Corinthians 13, Paul writes about doing great ministry for God while having little *hesed*. This description sounds a lot like what we heard Jesus say to the Ephesian church in Revelation:

> If I speak in the tongues of men or of angels, but do not have love, I am only a resounding gong or a clanging cymbal. If I have the gift of prophecy and can fathom all mysteries and all knowledge, and if I have a faith that can move mountains, but do not have love, I am nothing. If I give all I possess to the poor and give over my body to hardship that I may boast, but do not have love, I gain nothing. (vv. 1–3)

Until we restore our loving attachments to God and each other, we are wasting our time doing ministry, church, or anything else for that matter.

Paul is as blunt as Jesus is in Revelation 2. If we neglect *hesed*, we are a clanging cymbal. God plugs His ears. No matter how gifted and hardworking we might be, we are nothing. No matter how much we sacrifice and suffer for the gospel, we gain nothing. Until we restore our loving attachments to God and each other, we are wasting our time doing ministry, church, or anything else for that matter.

The Low-*Hesed* Church

Let's examine what low *hesed* looks like in the church. One result is a transactional culture. Relationships between leadership, staff, and volunteers are largely transactional and performance based. As long as you provide what the church wants, you are welcome and valued. If you no longer perform, you become invisible. Eventually you will be dismissed and forgotten. By definition, a performance-based relationship cannot be *hesed* because a main characteristic of *hesed* love is that it can survive bad performance and bad character. We don't kick our children out of the home when they misbehave. Our relationship is too strong.

Some church leaders have transactional management practices that guarantee low *hesed*. I have heard of churches that adopted the General Electric model of firing the lowest performing 10 percent of their staff each year. This is a practice that concretely assures a low level of *hesed* in the staff. All churches must dismiss staff occasionally, but when a staff member is dismissed, are they still treated like family, or does that bond disappear? Does leadership have an "out of sight, out of mind" view of relationships? Is there mourning and pain when someone leaves staff or leaves the church? Or do they just disappear? The spiritual damage done to discarded people echoes King David's complaint: "I am forgotten as though I were dead; I have become like broken pottery" (Ps. 31:12). When people are discarded because they are no longer useful, *hesed* is low.

Another form of low *hesed* is a friendly but loosely attached community. One of my professors in seminary would emphasize that a pastor must maintain a "collegial relationship" with the members of the church. This sets a low bar for the definition of *love*. Having weak *hesed* does not mean that the people in the community dislike each other. Shallow *hesed* means their love has weak sticking power and does not function as a family. Relationships are collegial.

Many churches are oriented in a way that makes *hesed* attachments difficult to build, so people remain acquaintances. Members know and enjoy each other, but they do not bond deeply. They operate at a comfortable distance. When people leave the community, they might just disappear. There might be some acknowledgment of their leaving, but there is little separation pain. They just move on. A low-*hesed* church may have a big front door and attract many new people, but the back door is just as big for those leaving. Large churches are especially vulnerable to this form of weak attachment, but we see it in all sizes of churches.

A high-*hesed* church is willing to accept pain and character flaws, realizing that with *hesed* comes pain, the pain of deep attachment. There is a reason why some communities stay weakly attached—to protect themselves from pain. When a member leaves a *hesed*-bonded community, it hurts like when a child leaves home. C. S. Lewis describes this avoidance of love in his book *The Four Loves*:

> To love at all is to be vulnerable. Love anything, and your heart will certainly be wrung and possibly be broken. If you want to make sure of keeping it intact, you must give your heart to no one, not even to an animal. Wrap it carefully round with hobbies and little luxuries; avoid all entanglements; lock it up safe in the casket or coffin of your selfishness. But in that casket—safe, dark, motionless, airless—it will change. It will not be broken; it will become unbreakable, impenetrable, irredeemable.[12]

Lewis understood the glue-like nature of love. When Paul informed the elders of the Ephesian church that they will never see him again, they were devastated. They experienced the attachment pain that Lewis describes. "They all wept as they embraced him and kissed him. What grieved them most was his statement that they would never see his face again" (Acts 20:37–38). This is a vivid picture of the beautiful pain of *hesed* attachment. Loosely connected communities and performance-based churches avoid pain by limiting attachment to each other, but they miss out on the extravagant family love of God.

Small groups are often seen as the solution to "creating community." However, *hesed* does not automatically grow in a small group. Leaders and members of the group need to be taught the importance of *hesed* and trained how to build it. The curriculum must make relationship-building a centerpiece of the group curriculum instead of an afterthought. I have been in many small groups, and the content usually consists of discussion questions from the Bible or the sermon. Practices that form the deep attachments of a spiritual family should also be intentionally included. Let me remind you again that without *hesed* attachments, our brain is not in the state where our character will respond to input. We stay the same, even as we discuss wonderful questions on last week's sermon.

Sometimes, the attachments in a small group will unintentionally have a growth spurt, often the result of suffering of one of the members of the group. A death, a divorce, or a sickness. You will hear people say, "Our group was never the same after that." This is good! However, it is even better to make *hesed* an intentional part of every small group.

The Importance of Imitation

In modern culture we do not think of imitation as the main way we form our character. Our churches are configured to deliver strong biblical teaching, sacraments, liturgy (in different forms), and worship. We are exhorted to follow Jesus, but few churches have strategies to mix mature Christians with younger Christians in a multi-maturity *hesed* community. Thus, we restrict the flow of sap that delivers the transformation Jesus described in John 15. The flow gets choked by two common strategies of modern churches.

First, as we have already seen, if our Christian communities do not stress the centrality of *hesed*, and our people are not trained to love, our attachments stay shallow. These weak bonds restrict the flow of character change. Second, we see churches organize not only small groups, but also most ministries around age groups. Elementary, middle school, high school, college, career, young married couples, middle age, elderly are all separated into their own groups. This creates communities where everyone is close to the same level of maturity. When newer Christians do not observe how a more mature disciple acts in different life situations, imitation does not get a chance to work its magic. Subdividing communities by life stage prevents the transmission of maturity.

Our right brain operates in the realm of relationships. Our relational experiences and memories mold our character. When we see a more mature person handling a difficult situation, that image gets processed in our relational brain. Our right brain absorbs this image of a mature Christian and goes to work on our character. All of this happens faster than conscious thought.

Let's suppose our small group arrives at the airport to discover that our flights have been canceled. I watch as our leader talks kindly to the airline employee. Suppose my previous image of handling a canceled flight was my father insulting the attendant. My brain makes the connection, "Oh! So this is how I am supposed to act when an airline cancels my flight at the last minute." My brain's identity center receives an update on how we handle canceled flights in the kingdom of God. Imitation is a direct driver of transformation, and it requires a *hesed* relationship to be the delivery pipeline.

I will let Jim explain in more detail how our brain uses imitation to form our character, both positively and negatively:

The right hemisphere is essentially nonverbal and operates by updating my reality and my response six times per second. If we tried to use words to run this fast-track system we could not even fit one word into each 1/6 of a second frame. What we can see in a sixth of a second is a picture. Thus, the answers of who I am and how I should act come from memory pictures we could call "examples." As we generate response options on the go we are essentially imitating examples we have seen. We can "see" examples by watching people but also by watching media and even reading or imagination. There is no chance to stop, talk, and create options in real time interactions. We imitate what we have seen—even when we swore we would never do what our parents did.

Jesus' entire ministry is an illustration of the importance of imitation. He is the perfect example of what it looks like to live in the kingdom of God. He showed His disciples how to handle praise and insults. He showed them how to suffer and how to bring healing. His disciples heard Him teach and also saw how He acted under pressure. What is our attitude toward inconvenient interruptions of our plans? How do I react to abandonment? What do I do when people praise me and want to promote me? How do I love people? He left us volumes of examples from His life.

Jesus exhorted His followers to imitate Him. After Jesus washed His disciples' feet, He said to them, "If I then, your Lord and Teacher, have washed your feet, you also ought to wash one another's feet. For I have given you an example, that you also should do just as I have done to you" (John 13:14–15 ESV). Notice that Jesus did not just give them a sermon on washing feet. He bent down and washed, giving them an image of what it looked like. The first thing we learn to imitate is His love: "A new commandment I give to you, that you love one another: just as I have loved you, you also are to love one another" (John 13:34 ESV). Jesus is saying to His disciples and to the rest of us, "Imitate Me."

Paul understands the transformative power of imitation when he writes, "Therefore I urge you to imitate me" (1 Cor. 4:16). He reminds the Corinthians later in the same letter, "Follow my example, as I follow the example of Christ" (11:1). Our attachments to Jesus and each other channel the flow of Christlike character— our instantaneous responses to the world around us.

Bracelets with "WWJD" were once popular among Christians. They were meant to be a reminder to slow down and think, *What would Jesus do?* Unfortunately, it is too late. Our embedded character has already acted by the time WWJD has time to arrive in my conscious mind. I have already acted when I start to think, *What would Jesus do?* Instead, we need to have robust practices of living in the presence of more mature Christians. We can also activate the circuitry of character formation by reliving memories and meditating on the behavior of Jesus and other mature Christians. You will get a chance to practice this at the end of the chapter.

The new believers in the city of Thessalonica saw how Paul lived his daily life among them. He was not idle but worked hard for his own provisions. He never ate someone's food without paying so as not to be a financial burden to them. They saw his maturity, and he explained, "We did this, not because we do not have the right to such help, but in order to offer ourselves as a model for you to imitate" (2 Thess. 3:9). To another community he wrote, "Join together in following my example, brothers and sisters, and just as you have us as a model, keep your eyes on those who live as we do" (Phil. 3:17).

The author of Hebrews exhorts his readers to think of their

spiritual leaders. "Consider the outcome of their way of life and imitate their faith" (13:7). We need good teaching, but we also need images. We need to see what it looks like to live in God's kingdom, and Jesus gave us both. We make a grave mistake when we think that teaching alone is sufficient. Our character is formed by imitating those to whom we are attached. Our brain processes images and memories of relational events to form our inner person. *Hesed* relationships are the conduit for the flow of these relational examples of mature character to a less mature person. No *hesed*, no fruit.

Building *Hesed*

By this time, you might be wondering, *Where does my Christian community stand? How much* hesed *is in our relational soil?* A good way to assess the *hesed* in your community is to look at leadership, money, staff, and time.

Are your leaders emotionally healthy people with good relational skills? Would you want to imitate them? Do they love people well, especially people who irritate them? How much time and money does your church spend developing loving attachments between your people? Does your church offer training on things like relational skills, emotional resilience, and character formation? Is love the starting point for every ministry and activity?

When you walk into a strongly attached community, you feel something in your body. "Wow! These people really love to be together!" High-*hesed* communities bring God's joy to people. This stimulates a hunger and desire to bond with God and others. Joy remains high, even in the presence of suffering because the community's bonds are stronger than their distress. In such communities, people are not afraid to reveal their weaknesses because they know that they will receive loving help. The ultimate proof that we are living in a high-*hesed* community is when we love our enemies.

A strongly attached church is viscerally different from a low-*hesed* church. A high-*hesed* church builds its life around joyful relationships. New believers are immediately drawn into a community of love. Parents are shown how to build *hesed* in their marriages and families. Attachments have priority.

Of the four ingredients in healthy relational soil, *hesed* will find the most resistance. The other three can be increased by intentional teaching and practices. *Hesed* is different because it requires restructuring how we think of church and the way we relate to each other. We must practice being a family; it doesn't happen automatically. *Hesed* must become part of our DNA.

A good place to start building *hesed* is by incorporating it into our values statement. A pastor friend in Kansas City adopted a value statement for his church saying, "We will never tax but only fuel the *hesed* in our community." Instead of *hesed* being an afterthought, it is the first thing they consider.

Another friend of mine helped craft the mission statement for his church: "Reaching Boulder with the gospel by becoming a place of relational connectedness and spiritual discovery."

We build *hesed* by reminding each other as a part of our community worship, and we emphasize *hesed* in every ministry. Although regularly declaring the importance of *hesed* will not create deep attachments on its own, it is a good first step.

Building joy in a community is another way to increase *hesed*. *Hesed* relationships also make a group joyful. Joy and *hesed* build each other in a cycle of mutual magnification. They were created to operate hand in hand. Joy and *hesed* are the first ingredients we add to improve our relational soil. These first two ingredients improve each other, and the subsequent two nutrients are ineffective without them.

Sharing food and drink together raises both joy and *hesed* in a community. Food was created for us to bond to God and each other. However, we need training, because eating does not automatically create *hesed*. Many of us have a habit of bonding with the food itself instead of the One who provided the food or the person who prepared it. Bonding with food leads to food addictions and unhealthy eating habits. When we bond with the food, we do not build our attachment with others at the table and God who provided the meal. For food to act as a bonding agent, we need good teaching and training in the community. Learning how to use food and drink to build our love for each other should be part of every church's discipleship program.

We see the importance of food in Jesus' life. After He called Matthew to be His disciple, we read, "While Jesus was having dinner at Matthew's house . . ." (Matt 9:10). The first thing Jesus did after starting a relationship with Matthew was have dinner with him.

Many of Jesus' famous teachings happened at the dinner table. In the book of Revelation, He offers reconciliation to a wandering church by offering a meal: "Here I am! I stand at the door and knock. If anyone hears my voice and opens the door, I will come in and eat with that person, and they with me" (3:20). Jesus shares food to repair damaged *hesed*.

Food is not the only thing we share that builds our bonds to each other. Sharing weakness is an essential practice that deepens our connections. Concealed weakness leads to shallow *hesed*. In a high-*hesed* community, everyone can share the difficult and vulnerable areas of their lives. We all have parts of our lives that we would prefer to keep in the dark. Being honest and open about our weaknesses is part of transformation.[13] Unlike our culture, which attaches around strengths, we, as followers of Jesus, attach around our weaknesses as well.

Our *hesed* with the Father lets us spill everything in our hearts to Him. "Trust in him at all times, you people; pour out your hearts to him, for God is our refuge" (Ps. 62:8). Our weaknesses are visible to God, and He is not shocked. Sick people, sinners, and failures flocked to Jesus because they sensed safety in His *hesed*. Our love should have the same magnetic attraction.

Jesus openly modeled how to share weakness. He experienced great distress the night He was handed over to be killed. He did not hide His pain from His disciples: "My soul is overwhelmed with sorrow to the point of death. Stay here and keep watch with me" (Matt. 26:38). Although Jesus never modeled character weakness—because, unlike us, He had none—He revealed His thirst, hunger, and having no place to lay His head, among other things.

Paul, the greatest church planter in the history of Christianity, was not an aloof visionary leader. He was deeply attached to his people and openly shared weakness. We see Paul's openness with the Corinthian church: "I came to you in weakness with great fear and trembling" (1 Cor. 2:3). Later in this same letter, he uses sarcasm to try to change their view of weakness. "We are fools for Christ, but you are so wise in Christ! We are weak, but you are strong! You are honored, we are dishonored!" (4:10). Paul writes in a second letter to the Corinthian church, "If I must boast, I will boast of the things that show my weakness" (2 Cor. 11:30). He repeatedly shares his weakness, hoping they will eventually learn from his example (1 Cor. 1:27; 2:3; 4:10; 9:22; 2 Cor. 4:7–11; 11:16–33; 12:1–10; 13:4, 9).

Paul gained his perspective on weakness from Jesus Himself. When Paul pleaded for the Lord to heal a painful affliction he was suffering, Jesus responded, "My grace is sufficient for you, for my power is made perfect in weakness." Paul understood and proclaimed, "Therefore I will boast all the more gladly about my weaknesses, so that Christ's power may rest on me. That is why, for Christ's sake, I delight in weaknesses, in insults, in hardships, in persecutions, in difficulties. For when I am weak, then I am strong" (2 Cor. 12:9–10).

Developing the trust needed to share and hear weakness requires courageous leaders who are willing to go first. Leaders must be tenacious because, like the Corinthian believers, we need to hear this more than once. Most of us have built-in reflexes to hide our blemishes and magnify our strengths. Leaders must show us how to share our flaws and receive the weakness of others with gentleness.

We follow Paul's example for people under our care, "But we were gentle among you, like a nursing mother taking care of her own children" (1 Thess. 2:7 ESV). As we read about sharing weaknesses, you may be thinking, *This is not safe in my church.* Unfortunately, you may be right. Too many churches are not safe places to build *hesed* by sharing failure. Many people are uncomfortable with their own debilities and have never learned to treat others' shame and struggles with tenderness. Revealing your failure may result in lots of "good advice," or even worse, condemnation.

If you have narcissists in your community, sharing weakness gives them ammunition. Narcissists pounce on the weaknesses of others to advance their own interests. We saw in chapter 3 that a narcissist in our community can rip a hole in our joy tank. Narcissistic influences will stamp out family bonding. *Hesed* is threatening to narcissists because they separate others in order to conquer. Strong *hesed* will neutralize this strategy.

Hesed and joy are the first two building blocks of a relational soil that is both transformational and resistant to narcissism. These two nutrients are indispensable. Our faces light up when we see each other, and our attachments to each other have sticking power. The quality of soil determines what will grow and what will not grow. Our next nutrient will provide a stable sense of who we are.

When we fail to build *hesed*, our churches do not function as spiritual families. Instead, churches become religious institutions with little power to transform lives. We have forgotten our first love, and our churches are in danger of no longer being Christian (even though they might have excellent doctrine). When our relational soil lacks joy and *hesed*, we fulfill the great omission that Dallas Willard decried. When we build joy and *hesed* into our soil, we reverse this decline and are on our way to becoming abundantly fruitful.

GROUP DISCUSSION QUESTIONS

1. Complete the *Soil Sample 2:* Hesed *Attachment Development* in Appendix A for your Christian community. Discuss your *hesed* level.
2. Rewrite the following Scriptures, replacing "love" with the concept of a family level attachment.
   a. "A new command I give you: Love one another. As I have loved you, so you must love one another" (John 13:34)
   b. "Above all, love each other deeply, because love covers over a multitude of sins" (1 Peter 4:8).
3. In Colossians 2:2, Paul prays for his readers that their hearts may be "encouraged, being knit together in love" (ESV). What can you do in your church or small group to knit yourselves together in a closer bond of love?
4. What can you do in your Christian community to practice sharing weaknesses on a regular basis? What are the dangers

of sharing weakness? How can you create a safe environment for presenting your true selves, including your character flaws?

TRY IT OUT

1. Spend two minutes in silence thinking about Jesus and you being a vine and a branch. Use your imagination and meditate on this picture Jesus gave us of His closeness. Write down any thoughts you want to share with your group.
2. Read Matthew 8:23–25. Jesus is doing something that most of us cannot—sleeping in the midst of chaos. Learn to imitate Jesus by meditating on this story for a few minutes in silence, letting your mind absorb the calm that Jesus models while everyone else is panicking.
3. Practice sharing and receiving weakness in order to deepen *hesed*. Go around the circle and share the following:
   a. A physical weakness (a sore knee, a cold, a headache). Everyone responds to the person's weakness by saying together, "Lord Jesus, help us." Repeat until everyone has had a chance.
   b. A relationship weakness (broken friendship, marriage problem, family problem). Everyone responds to the person sharing, "Lord Jesus, help us." Repeat until every one has had a chance.
   c. Sharing a character weakness is the most vulnerable, but it is essential in forming our character. For this step, share a low-or medium-level character flaw.
      i. Spend one minute in silence asking Jesus to show you something He likes about you.
      ii. Spend another minute asking Him to reveal a character weakness He wants you to share with the group.

iii. Go around the circle and share something about your self that God enjoys. Then something about your character that God would like you to work on to change.

iv. Everyone responds by saying, "Lord Jesus, help us." Do not comment or give advice.

FURTHER RESOURCES FOR THIS CHAPTER

Relational and emotional brain skills:

- See thrivetoday.org/thrive
- Chris M. Coursey, *Transforming Fellowship: 19 Brain Skills That Build Joyful Community*

Healing trauma:

- Wilder, Kang, Loppnow, Loppnow, *Joyful Journey: Listening to Immanuel*
- E. James Wilder and Chris M. Coursey, *Share Immanuel: The Healing Lifestyle*
- The extensive writings and videos of Karl D. Lehman, MD, at KCLehman.com; this material is more technical than that in *Joyful Journey.*

Building community:

- Tom Anthony, *Building Better Community*

The problem of narcissism:

- E. James Wilder, *The Pandora Problem*

The importance of *hesed*:

- Wilder, *The Pandora Problem*, especially chapter 1
- E. James Wilder and Marcus Warner, *The Solution of Choice*

5

Group Identity: What Kind of People Are We?

*Therefore, as God's chosen people, holy and dearly
loved, clothe yourselves with compassion, kindness,
humility, gentleness and patience.*

Colossians 3:12

AS I GOT INVOLVED in the Christian group at the university, I quickly realized that I was in for some surprises. The people in my new community looked at life differently from how I did. Their values were different. One night, my roommate, Steve, and I were studying together, and we needed a break. So we started talking. Somehow, the topic of sex came up, probably because I said something inappropriate. After all, I was only a two-month-old Christian. My comment had something to do with having sex before marriage, which I thought was perfectly normal behavior. Steve looked at me and calmly said, "Michel, we as Christians look at sex very differently from what you are probably used to hearing." He was right. I grew up in a house full of pornography. This was the pre-internet age, and my father had subscriptions to several pornographic magazines. He never threw the magazines away. Instead, he stacked them up in his office in the basement, right next to my bedroom. This was my first exposure to sex as a young man.

Steve's comment piqued my curiosity, so I asked him to explain the Christian view of sex. My best recollection of what he said is, "God has a high view of sex because it is so special. With most special things, we put careful protections around them. God does that with sex. He created sex for marriage—and marriage alone—as a blessing on His beautiful creation of man and woman. So Christians wait until marriage to enjoy sex."

I could not stop my instantaneous reaction. "Steve, that is ridiculous! No one believes that! I have never heard that view of sex in my life." I was not lying. My view of sex was shaped by a combination of my friends from school, television, movies, and the seductive pages of pornography.

Steve was not flustered by my outburst. He calmly replied, "Continue reading the Bible, and see what you learn about God's perspective on sex. Let's keep talking about this."

I did not realize at the time that I was getting an education in group identity. Steve was teaching me how my new people think and act. I was in the middle of a massive group identity earthquake that would reshape my core beliefs and behaviors. I had many similar encounters with my new group identity over the following years. My new people invited me into their community, and God used them to change me, step by step, from the inside out.

Group identity is not a common term for most Christians, but it plays a crucial and overlooked role in transformation. Group identity forms our character. Identity formation is a big hole in spiritual formation.

The church over the centuries has appealed to creeds. Creeds answer the question, "As followers of Jesus, what do we believe?" Group identity statements are similar, but they define character. Instead of focusing primarily on what we believe, group identity answers the questions, "As followers of Jesus, what kind of people are we? How do the people of God act?"

In Western culture, identity is individualistic. In other cultures, identity is naturally thought of in terms of group values. Through infancy and childhood, the brain is designed to develop individual identity through attachment to the parents and other caregivers. Around age twelve, the brain undergoes a structural change that balances individual identity with group identity. From this point on, our group identity is a key player in the formation of character. We are formed by our strongest attachments and the shared identity of our community. Our brains are wired this way. Let's look at how Jesus, the One who designed our brains, used group identity.

Group Identity in the Bible

When Jesus began His public ministry, He started by preaching, "Repent, for the kingdom of heaven is at hand" (Matt. 4:17 ESV). Jesus came to bring God's kingdom to earth and fill it with new citizens who live differently in this present age. Our salvation introduces us into a new kingdom, and we learn to live according to its values. Kingdom living requires changes in our character. Peter heard Jesus proclaim the new kingdom, and he never forgot this powerful truth. Many years later, he wrote to Christians, "But you are a chosen people, a royal priesthood, a holy nation, God's special possession" (1 Peter 2:9). Chosen, royal, holy, special. These strong words describe a new people inhabiting God's kingdom.

Jesus Himself lived out of a strong identity, and He taught it to

His disciples. In the Sermon on the Mount, Jesus delivers a heavy dose of group identity for a chosen, royal, holy, special people. He answers the questions: What kind of people are we? How do we act as members of God's kingdom on earth? Here are some examples of our group identity according to Jesus' sermon in Matthew 5–7.

> **We are a people who . . .**
> *take God's commands seriously.*
> *reconcile as quickly as possible.*
> *are careful to obey God in our sexuality, even with*
>   *glances and thoughts.*
> *remain faithful to our spouses.*
> *keep our word and have no need to make oaths.*
> *love our enemies and pray for them.*
> *seek to be rewarded by God instead of by people.*
> *forgive others because we have been forgiven so much*
>   *by our Father.*

The identity statements above are just a sample. In the Sermon on the Mount, Jesus unveils a beautiful description of what kind of people live in God's kingdom, although our world is still broken and confused. Notice that He primarily expounds on what kind of people we are and how we live. How do God's children act when we are angry with someone? How do we respond to financial problems? How do we treat a person when we see a flaw in their character? Jesus is building a strong base of identity to help His chosen people know what kind of people they are. He understands that His followers will need to know—and often be reminded of—who they are. When we forget, we start acting like salt that has lost its flavor (Matt. 5:13).

Paul's letters address at length not only what we believe but also how we act in our new kingdom. In Ephesians 5:8, Paul reminds us of the change in our group identity as a result of knowing Christ. "For you were once darkness, but now you are light in the Lord. Live as children of light." These words helped me understand the identity shift I experienced as a new believer in my Christian community. My roommate, Steve, was teaching me to live as a child of light.

The apostle Paul touches on many areas of our lives that will need transformation now that we live in God's kingdom. Notice how specific he is in Ephesians chapter 5:

We are a people who . . .
walk in love, just like Christ, because it is sweet perfume to God.
are careful with our sexuality and money because these easily corrupt us.
are careful with our words and jokes.
diligently find out what pleases God.
avoid and expose the works of darkness.
use our time carefully here on earth, making the most of every opportunity.
do not get drunk but are filled with the Spirit.
sing to each other and make up songs that connect us to each other and God.
always give thanks to God for everything.

In Colossians 3:12, Paul writes a general identity statement that every Christian community can work into their relational soil:

"Therefore, as God's chosen people, holy and dearly loved . . ."
[This is the new people we are in God's kingdom.]

113

"Clothe yourselves with compassion, kindness, humility, gentleness and patience."
[This is how we act as God's people.]

We will see in the next section that when we stop clothing ourselves with compassion, kindness, humility, gentleness, and patience, it reveals that we have forgotten who we are. We have identity amnesia. We are no longer acting like Christians.

Group Identity and the Brain

Our brains were designed to respond to group identity in order to help us act like "our people." Our right brain contains the control center that interprets our group identity and uses it to shape our inner character. The orbital prefrontal cortex (on the right side of my brain behind my eye) is dominant for integrating my current situation in life with who I am—in real time. Every one-sixth of a second our right brain tries to answer the questions, "Who am I? How do my people act now?" If my control center is working smoothly, my circumstances are integrated with my group identity. I spontaneously act with joy and peace. If my control center desynchronizes, I forget who I am and how to connect with those around me. I stop acting like myself. Even though I am a Christian, I stop acting like one. My brain has cramped. I no longer act with compassion, kindness, humility, gentleness, and patience.

If I am not a part of a high-joy *hesed* community with a strong group identity, I will not know how to change my behavior. My own willpower will be insufficient to prevent me from acting in non-Christian ways. This response happens faster than conscious thought. It is my reflex reaction to distress. For example, if I lash out in anger, the effective strategy to change this flaw in my character is not to try harder next time it happens. Instead, I must focus on changing my instantaneous reflex reactions when under distress. Again, this is not done by direct willpower.

We define character as our embedded automatic responses to our relational environment, our instantaneous behavior that flows naturally from our heart. Changing our "faster than conscious" behaviors sounds strange to Western ears. I needed several explanations from Jim before I understood what he was saying. We emphasize the importance of willpower in Western culture. A typical modern strategy to correct a flaw in our character is to try harder.

When we understand how God designed our brains, we can see that willpower is too far downstream to directly influence reflex reactions. Our willpower is good at cleaning up when we make a mess. We apologize and reconcile the relationship. Willpower also helps us create strategies that will indirectly change our instantaneous reactions in the future. This is where we must engage our willpower indirectly. Direct willpower has little effect on our character.

Direct willpower has little effect on our character.

Group identity has the power to change character because it operates in the fast-track on the right spot in the brain. Our automatic responses to distress (faster than conscious thought) can be trained by our group identity. Let me state this again because this concept is countercultural. Our instantaneous reactions to life's circumstances (some of which result in non-Christian behavior) can be transformed by having a joyful *hesed* community that has a well-developed group identity based in the character of Jesus.

Character is revealed by how we act instinctively to our relational surroundings. As our group identity sinks into our hearts, and we learn the correction techniques in the next chapter, we will naturally start exhibiting transformed character. Spontaneously. The people with whom we share joy, *hesed*, and belonging change us outside the realm of our direct willpower. We are changed by training the prefrontal cortex in our right brain.

In our misdirected emphasis on willpower, we read the group identity Scriptures in the Sermon on the Mount and treat them as rules that we must follow. We think that we learn to obey Jesus by trying hard. When this does not work, we grit our teeth and try harder. This was my strategy for most of my Christian life. If we look at Jesus, He naturally reacted to His surroundings with behavior that exhibited kingdom living. He was not gritting His teeth. His character flowed from His heart, so He always acted like Himself in all circumstances:

When He was criticized and attacked.

When people engulfed Him and followed Him everywhere.

When the crowds deserted Him.

When His closest friends stood by Him.

When they abandoned Him.

When Jesus was hanging on the cross and His life was slowly draining away, He made sure someone would take care of His mother. This is how a child of God acts.

Shallow Group Identity

Even if we have a high-joy community with strong *hesed* attachments, we still need to develop a deep-rooted group identity as a part of our discipleship. We see a kingdom group identity in Jesus' teaching. We see it in the rest of the New Testament writings. Unfortunately, too many Christian communities have poorly developed group identities. We have not done the hard work in the right places. If we fail to develop our group identity, our character remains untouched by much of our Christian practice. Our brains are wired to respond to group identity, but churches often do not give our brains what they need to transform us. This is why left-brained Christianity produces so little transformation.

Our understanding of group identity has undergone great changes in the last hundred years. It used to be common to live in neighborhoods and towns where the people around us knew not only us but also our parents and grandparents. It would be common to hear stories of our grandparents, and they would teach us about their character, for better or worse. Now we live in a disconnected and compartmentalized culture.

I left the neighborhood in which I grew up to go to college, where few people knew me and none knew my parents. I started over. After college, I got a job in a different city from where I grew up. During this time, my parents moved from our neighborhood in Denver to the East Coast. No one knew who they were. My family history of disconnection is typical in the Western world.

This family fragmentation weakens the development of group identity in the culture at large. I am no longer told who I am in a multigenerational community. These changes in our society lead to a shallow identity. When Christian communities follow this cultural trend, we also end up with shallow identities. Instead of standing out as lights in a dark world, we blend in.

Many churches can state their values: Christ-centered, biblical authority, community, discipleship, evangelism. We wish these values could reach our group identity. Many denominations have defined their group identities around doctrine. We are: Reformed, charismatic, Orthodox, Catholic, or evangelical. The problem is that what we believe has not been that effective in changing how we act. Along with the apostles' doctrine we need the apostles' character.

Some churches form their group identity around their ministry activities or styles: "We are a liturgical church. We are an inner city church. We are a church for the lost and broken." Others derive their identity from the fame and personality of their pastor. "I go to Jim Smith's church!" Personality-based churches are a shallow attempt to form group identity. Christ's character is still not actively in the center.

Toxic Group Identity

Toxic group identity can also corrupt a Christian community by forming bad character instead of Christlike character. Paul gives us an example of corrupted group identity when he had to correct a cult of personality in the Corinthian church:

> *My brothers and sisters, some from Chloe's household have informed me that there are quarrels among you. What I mean is this: One of you says, "I follow Paul"; another, "I follow Apollos"; another, "I follow Cephas"; still another, "I follow Christ."*
>
> *Is Christ divided? Was Paul crucified for you? Were you baptized in the name of Paul? . . .*
>
> *For when one says, "I follow Paul," and another, "I follow Apollos," are you not mere human beings?*
>
> *What, after all, is Apollos? And what is Paul? Only servants, through whom you came to believe—as the Lord has assigned to each his task. I planted the seed, Apollos watered it, but God has been making it grow. So neither the one who plants nor the one who waters is anything, but only God, who makes things grow. (1 Cor. 1:11–13; 3:4–7)*

When we identify with the fame and personality of our leader, our group identity gets corrupted. We lose touch with our true identity as followers of Jesus. Our group identity becomes toxic.

Group identities can also form around our pain, addictions, and trauma. We can mistake our malfunctions as our identity. *I am an alcoholic. I am a lost and broken person. I'm a sex addict. I keep having affairs because I'm addicted to love.* These are all statements I heard as a pastor. It is healthy to confess our malfunctions to each other, but it does harm to equate them to our identity. Our malfunctions are examples of when we *forget* to act like ourselves. As Christians, our identity is found in the perfect and beautiful character of Jesus.

When churches fail to develop a group identity in their people, other influences will fill this void. Big personalities. The surrounding culture. Political parties. Work environment. Satan can corrupt the beautiful things of God. Group identity will form us whether we realize it or not.

We must caution you that group identity can be used for evil as well as good. The Nazis developed a strong group identity in their people. A twisted group identity will produce crooked character. One can imagine Nazis saying to each other, "Stop showing compassion to those Jewish people. We are a people who exterminate detestable people like these Jews." We should not be surprised how often tyrants and evil ideas create strong group identities. Group power to impact character cannot be overlooked.

Building Healthy Group Identity

Churches should be driven by one personality—the personality of Christ. The rest of us are simple servants who humbly fulfill tasks the Lord has assigned to us. Jesus instructs us well: "So you also, when you have done everything you were told to do, should say, 'We are unworthy servants; we have only done our duty'" (Luke 17:10).

Building a group identity around the character of Jesus

requires commitment from leadership. Our group identity must be so integral that it comes out of our pores. Leaders must offer a robust development of identity that can handle a wide range of life and situations. The leader must provide intentional practices that work the identity into the soil.

One way a community can build a strong character identity is by speaking regularly to each other about what kind of people we are. Some traditions recite doctrinal statements as part of their Christian practice. We also need to do the same with how we live. We need constant reminders.

Our group identity must reflect the multifaceted character of Jesus. He was not boring and two-dimensional. The character of some Christians would make you think Jesus was a dull fellow. Healthy group identity glows, revealing the beautiful colors of the kingdom of God. We often pay attention to our doctrine and teaching. In many ways, this is good and necessary. The apostle Paul exhorts a young pastor to "watch your life and doctrine closely" (1 Tim. 4:16). Yet many of us rarely perform more than a cursory examination of our lives. We might watch for the obvious flaws: addictions, adultery, immorality, and dishonesty. These failures are the product of numerous flaws that went undetected. We need to catch little things before they metastasize. Here are examples:

You start to drink several cocktails after dinner in your office with the door closed since you lost your job. When your spouse knocks on the door, you pretend to be searching for jobs.

You feel attracted to a person you saw in the gym and find yourself thinking about him/her.

You feel an urge to click on a link on your computer that will lead you down a dark road.

Your spouse complains about an argument he or she had with a friend, and you think, *How silly.*

You fill most of your free time looking at your phone and surfing social media.

Your neighbor constantly parks his car in front of your house, and you imagine how to get revenge.

You avoid deeper community because you are just too tired. You would rather relax and watch a movie.

You walk away from an argument with your spouse and never try to resolve it.

You insist on winning an argument with your spouse, even if it requires you to say "ridiculous things."

We can all identify with these examples. Many of our behaviors are overlooked, but they reveal that we forget who we are. Underneath these forgetful moments are subtle distortions in our identities and values. Below that, unhealed wounds fester and contaminate our identities. Left untreated, these ignored flaws can blow up our relational lives. We all have this subterranean identity battle raging.

A robust group identity helps us nip our flaws in the bud. The roots of our group identity deepen and spread when we remind each other who we are. Regular reminders ground our identity in the character of Jesus. We need to tell each other what kind of people we are, not only as a reminder but also to immerse new Christians into their new identities. New members will need to have their group identities updated like I did when I was nineteen years old.

A church that is serious about the Great Commission will dedicate a part of their Sunday service to building and maintaining group identity. This practice must become an integral part of our spiritual formation trainings, weekly meetings, and small groups.

My Personal Example

Our basement started filling up with people as friends invited friends. We crowded into couches and sat on the floor as Jim trained us to activate the character-forming capacity of our brains. Our exercises included building our group identity. Every week, we started our meeting with an identity statement, and we closed our meeting by repeating the identity statement. Here are a few examples:

"We are a people who would rather listen than speak."

"We are a people who see what God is building in others."

"We are a people who spontaneously love our enemies and return blessings for cursings."

"We are a people who remind each other who we really are whenever we forget."

"We are a people who share other's pain, even when we have caused it."

(From *The Pandora Problem* exercises)

I imagined going to a church where we remind each other of what kind of people we are. We get specific. How do I act when I get a speeding ticket? How do I act when I lose my job? How do I act when I get a promotion? In all of these situations and more, we ask, "How do the people of God behave here? What does it look like to live in the kingdom of God in this situation?" We are careful to include our most forgetful areas of life, when we most easily stop acting like Christians.

We treat people as obstacles to our advancement.

We make solving problems more important than relationships.

We argue loudly with someone who disagrees with our politics.

We see a leader insulting a person behind their back, and we say nothing.

The first area to target for a strong group identity is our relational soil. A church that transforms the character of its people agrees on the importance of joy and *hesed*. Jesus was a man of deep *hesed* and joy, so our identities possess these traits.

When we grow *hesed* and joy, we look people in the eyes. We regularly remind each other who we are, and our group identity statements fortify our relational soil. "We are a people who are happy to be together, and we create environments of joyful belonging." "We are a people who value relationships above performance or productivity." "We are a people who are faithful friends. I will not abandon you, even when we have a conflict." I want to live in that community! Do you?

In the next chapter, we will look at what we do when we forget our identity. When I stop acting like myself, my community needs to help me. Group identity alone is not enough to transform our character. We need another essential skill.

■ ‑ ■ ‑ ■ ‑ ■ ‑ ■ ‑ ■ ‑ ■ ‑ ■ ‑ ■ ‑ ■ ‑ ■ ‑ ■ ‑ ■ ‑ ■ ‑ ■ ‑ ■ ‑ ■ ‑ ■

When we fail to build the character of Christ into the identity of our community, we easily forget who we are. We become salt that's not salty, and our character lacks the savory flavor of transformation. When our relational

soil lacks joy, *hesed*, and group identity, we often stop acting like Jesus. A well-developed group identity will prepare our soil for transformation.

- -

GROUP DISCUSSION QUESTIONS

1. Complete the Soil Sample 3: Group Identity Strength in Appendix A for your Christian community. Discuss the strength of your community's group identity.
2. Read 1 Peter 5:8–9.
   a. What reason does Peter give for enduring?
   b. Why would knowing of the suffering of other Christians help us suffer?
   c. As a group, create a group identity statement about how we deal with Satan's attacks.
   d. As a group, create a group identity statement about how we suffer. We are a people who _____.
3. Read Matthew 7:3–5 and come up with a group identity statement from this teaching. We are a people who _____.

TRY IT OUT

1. As a group, read the following group identity statement out loud to each other: "We are a people who get our group identity from the character of Jesus."
2. Read Colossians 3:12. Think of a recent time when you failed to act with "*compassion, kindness, humility, gentleness and patience.*" Create a group identity statement to remind you who you are in that situation. Have the group read each person's reminder back to them.

3. Develop your group's identity by repeating the above two practices the next five times you meet. Have someone in the group compile your identity statement list as it grows. This list will help you practice what you learn in the next chapter.

FURTHER RESOURCES FOR THIS CHAPTER

Group identity:

• E. James Wilder, *The Pandora Problem*, especially chapter 14

6

· · · · · · · · · ·

Healthy Correction: Stop Being So Nice

Whoever heeds life-giving correction will
be at home among the wise.

Proverbs 15:31

WHEN THE RELATIONAL soil of our community has been fortified with joy, *hesed*, and group identity, we really grow. If these three nutrients were all Jim had taught me, my life and community would have improved immensely. But making every plant grow like crazy does not give us the harvest we want. Jim told me how his father had poured a bag of nitrogen fertilizer on his lima beans. The plants grew up the wall and over the roof of the house. They were the biggest, greenest plants the neighborhood had ever seen. But they never yielded a bean. A critical nutrient was missing.

With our three essential nutrients, we would still see amazing growth but find some deformed tomatoes scattered in our crops. The fourth building block of healthy soil corrects our group identity where it has broken down. Even with an abundant supply of relational joy, *hesed*, and group identity, we must be careful what we grow. Group identity can grow bad fruit as well as good. We can live in joyful *hesed* and fail to act according to the character of Jesus. Our group identity breaks down, and we stop acting like ourselves. What do we do then?

The fourth soil ingredient targets malfunctions. We need to be corrected at times. We are going to look at the neurological mechanics of receiving and giving correction. Correction is easy to do incorrectly.

The Brain Science of Character

You have noticed that I have written a lot about character in this book. We are now at a place where we can incorporate what we have learned so far to present a thorough definition. Jim explains that character lies at the intersection of identity and values. For the brain, these activities converge in the prefrontal cortex (PFC). "The right prefrontal cortex is dominant for combining our values into our known responses. In particular, the ventromedial section of the PFC will seek the least damaging response to any situation. Character is the combination of our known responses (what people have done in the past) and our values (what our people prefer to do). We must eliminate the many responses that our people would not value."

In layman's terms, our character draws from two libraries: (1) our life history of observed responses of how to act, and (2) the values of "our people." Our brain scans both of these libraries to form our spontaneous behavior. The prefrontal cortex accesses the library of our observed examples and eliminates options that are contrary to our values. When *examples from my past* match *my current values* my brain has found *the winning options*.

Let's return to my conversation with Steve about sex. We were taking a study break when I asked him to explain the Christian view. Steve presented a very different group identity (a new set of values) from what I expected. I was blindsided. My reaction was cognitive dissonance—"This is ridiculous!" My two libraries contained the following value: "It is normal and healthy to have sex outside of marriage." My library up to this point contained examples from my family, community, television, movies, and porn that supported this value.

Now I was exposed to new values from someone I trusted and loved. I had never heard the Christian perspective on sexual behavior. Unknown to me, I was in the throes of having my character changed.

That semester, I also started hearing stories from other men in my group. They shared how they were learning to bring their sexual lives into alignment with the kingdom of God. They were honest, and they shared their temptations and failures, too. All of this was new to me. Both of my libraries were being updated simultaneously.

From the range of possibilities (observed responses on file in my mind), the prefrontal cortex must now figure out the least harmful option to my people. The catch comes in who we consider as "my people" because causing damage to "not my people" is not a problem.

Previous to my conversion, no Christian had been a member of "my people." My prefrontal cortex selected the observed behaviors and values that were stored so far, and produced the result: *sex outside of marriage is normal and healthy.* I did not realize at the time that, due to my new Christian community, my libraries were undergoing a massive update.

A common misunderstanding is that our character is defined mostly by moral truth and choices. When we see a flaw in a person's character, we think, "They do not understand God's teaching and are making bad choices." It is true that bad choices were involved, but the root impetus of our character lies elsewhere. In order to improve our behavior, we need to change our values and update our stored examples of how our people act. We cannot change our values directly. We must get them from our community, our group identity.

I need a Christ-centered *hesed* community to help me act more like Jesus. This community must have people who are more mature than I, because I need to update my library with their better examples. I need to see other people living in alignment with God's kingdom in areas where my libraries have not yet been updated. I also need to hear about "our values" from my community, how we act in this world as followers of Jesus. As you already know from the previous chapter, this is our group identity.

> **This community must have people who are more mature than I, because I need to update my library with their better examples.**

Now we can see that character is a collection of observed responses to various life situations that is quickly filtered through the options that my people value. The possibilities are ranked according to what would be the least damaging to my people. The brain formulates the options before we are conscious of them, although sorting out the least harmful may take longer.

Shame

Before we talk about how we can improve our character as a community, we need to talk about shame, one of the big six emotions. These six emotions are hardwired in the brain. This section may be hard for you to swallow. It was hard for me when I first heard Jim talk about shame. I urge you to persevere until the end. *Shame* is one of the most misunderstood words in the church and in our culture. We have an allergic reaction to shame for good reason. For most of us, if we look back over our lives, our experiences of shame felt toxic and harmful, and we thought, *I never want to feel that again.* We conclude that shame is something to be avoided. We arrange our lives with strategies that keep shame as far away as possible.

Brain science tells a more nuanced story than "shame equals bad." I can still remember when Jim first explained the neuroscience of shame. He said neuroscience reveals that shame is necessary for character to change. Our brain has dedicated circuits for handling shame, and they are tied to other circuits that control the formation of character. Shame is important for socialization, and without it, our character will not change.

Many of us were dumbfounded. What Jim was saying disagreed with everything we had heard about shame. We believed that shame was always satanic in nature and should be rejected. Jim said that to expand our understanding of shame, we need to know that there are two types of shame: toxic and healthy.

To understand healthy shame, we need to look at the unhealthy counterpart first.[1] Toxic shame communicates the message "you are bad." The message does not invite a way out of your "badness." It leaves you in shame with no solution or help. Toxic shame is connected to a conscious, almost always verbal message. These can come in many forms: you are stupid, worthless, ugly, disgusting, fat, skinny, slow, clumsy. Since a toxic shame is accompanied by a conscious message ("You will always be a loser"), it has a large left-brain component. If we validate the message ("You are right, I will always be a loser"), we feel worse. Our validation magnifies the shameful distress.

Healthy shame is a nonverbal spontaneous reaction to a face that is not happy to be with me. Healthy shame is the opposite of joy. We detect shame primarily from facial cues and voice tone. My right brain can tell from your face that I have lowered your joy. We can learn to be relational in shame, so healthy shame does not leave me alone. A healthy shame message is of the form, "I love you but believe that you stopped acting like yourself. Let me remind you how we act in this situation." Our *hesed* helps us regulate the emotional energy of shame. Without *hesed*, shame will push us to isolate and hide, which naturally sinks us into unhealthy shame. Most of us never learned to experience shame and stay relationally connected.

Shame and Correction

For some of us, staying relational in shame seems impossible. That was my first reaction to Jim's new perspective. I knew toxic shame would never improve character. Could the kind of reproof Jesus used involve healthy shame?

We can distinguish the two types of correction by whether or not the relationship is affirmed. Are we going to use shame to bring us together or push us apart? Toxic shame leaves us alone in our shame. Someone points out our failure and leaves us there. An example of toxic shame is the football coach yelling at one of his players because he got into a pushing match on the field. The referee calls a penalty, and a twenty-yard gain becomes a fifteen-yard loss. The coach yells in the player's face. The veins in the coach's neck pop out. And then he stomps away and thinks about the next play to call. The player stands on the sideline feeling alone and in shame. No character was formed that day. We all have experienced toxic shame growing up, with parents, siblings, friends, coaches, and teachers.

I was an easily distracted young kid. In my fifth grade English class, we had to hand in a five-page assignment. Not paying attention, I stapled the pages together without realizing that two of them were upside down and one was backwards. Later that day, the teacher called me up to her desk in front of the whole class. In a loud voice, she said, "Look at the quality of your work! It's upside down. Backwards! That is your life. You are backwards and upside down!" She slammed my paper down on her pile, and that was the end of the conversation. I was left to take the walk of shame back to my desk. Most of us have had experiences of toxic shame, many of them much worse than this example.

Correcting someone using healthy shame is couched in relationship. When I use shame in a healthy way, I always affirm the relationship above the problem. Once the security of our attachment is understood by both of us, I address the problem. Instead of just saying "you!" I also say "we," which affirms our group identity. We are in this together. I do not leave you alone in your shame. In effect, I communicate, "You have forgotten who you are. Let me remind you who we are. We are a people who _____. I would love to help you with this."

Most of us have never heard anything like that.

Let's revisit the example of the football error from above. Let's say I'm the coach and yell, "Why did you push that guy? You just lost us a good gain, and we may lose this game because of you! That was a stupid thing to do!" Then I stomp away angry. How would you feel? Alone. Dumb. You are thinking that maybe I have given up on you. You would like to hide.

Let's rewind. If I understand how the brain metabolizes shame relationally to form our character, this episode would look very different. First, I would simply look you in the eyes. No words. My eyes would say, "Our relationship is not at risk, even though you messed up." Then I would say, "You seem to have forgotten that we are not the kind of team that gets into little pushing matches when our feelings get hurt. Instead, we are learning to be men of character who can take an insult and walk away because our team is more important. This is a great opportunity for you to learn. Don't waste it."

Can you feel the difference?

Healthy shame affirms the relationship, points out how I am not acting like myself, and reaffirms who we really are, our group identity. I am being corrected but quickly invited back into my true identity. I feel the shame of my failure, but I am not left there long. I think, *I do not want to do that again.* I am immediately reminded of who I really am. I simply forgot and stopped acting like myself.

When a church believes that all shame is bad, we are depriving our community of a strong driver of character change. We either avoid giving reprimands altogether, or we try to correct people without shame. In our training with Jim, we all pushed back when he started talking about shame, but he was adamant. He replied bluntly, "Without shame (the sense that we are displeasing people) our character has zero motivation to change."

This was so new to us that I asked him to explain again. He said that there is a lovely little system in our brain, just above our right ear, that determines whether we are going to make a change. The brain corrects problems only if they cause discomfort—that is, some kind of pain. For the brain, the right saying would be "no pain, no change."

The bigger question revolves around "why shame?" There are seven kinds of relational pain wired into the brain.[2] Like all kinds of pain, these are both a warning that something is going wrong and a signal to make a corrective change. The common problem is that we try to stop the pain without making the relational repair that would correct the cause of the pain. This is like taking the battery out of the smoke alarm to stop the noise but not finding out why that alarm is sounding and correcting the problem.

Shame, then, is the pain signal related to our character and behavior when our behavior becomes something others want to avoid. Toxic shame (toxic shame gets most of the attention in the public mind) happens when we are told that there is a problem ("we don't like your character right now") but no relational solution is provided. Without a relational solution, people will eventually try to silence the pain with something. The common ways to pull the battery out of our emotional alarm are what we call addictions.

Healthy shame lets us learn character when it is combined immediately with a relational solution. Relational pain signals need relational solutions.

When we practiced using healthy shame in the training in our basement, we began to understand what he was saying, but we still implored him to use another word. In our culture, the word *shame* is loaded down with negative connotations and triggers negative responses in people. Why not choose another word for healthy shame, like *conviction*?

Jim said that the real problem is that, in our culture and up-bringing, a good use for shame has not gotten programmed into our bodies as something beneficial. When a culture does not give us a complete picture of shame, this leaves a hole in our emotional development. We are emotionally underdeveloped and do not know how to use this feeling. Shame is hardwired in our brains, so we must learn what to do with it.

Other emotions are hardwired, too—like fear. We do not avoid the word *fear*—although some of us do avoid it. Why should we avoid *shame*? We need to expand our understanding and ability to process shame. This is a normal skill we learn in a full-brained development. We train to metabolize the six big emotions: sadness, fear, anger, disgust, despair, and shame.

Shame is just a signal—an "I'm not bringing you joy" signal.

Handling shame in a healthy way protects the joy in our community. We are protecting *joy*, the first nutrient in our relational soil. A community that builds joy uses correction not only to build character, but also to maintain the joy level of the group. Unlike toxic shame, when we accept healthy shame, we feel better and our relationships are strengthened.

Do you have a strong negative reaction to hearing the word *shame*? If so, your family and community did not show you how to handle it. Toxic shame says, "You are a rotten person." Your shame training thus far has taught you a lie, not who you really are. This lack of emotional training is the real problem. We will see in chapter 8 that a full-brained discipleship program will train you to handle shame by restoring your true identity.

Reject Condemnation

If we want our families and churches to be transformational environments, we need to clearly distinguish between toxic and healthy shame. We need training on how to handle both types of shame. We must deal resolutely with toxic shame. The Christlike response to toxic shame is a firm rejection. Condemnation is the most common form of a toxic shame message, and we refuse to accept any form of condemnation. Toxic shame is never from God, so we must learn to protect ourselves from it.

Paul rejects condemnation in the life of a Christian: "Therefore, there is now no condemnation for those who are in Christ Jesus" (Rom. 8:1). Later in the same chapter, he writes, "Who will bring any charge against those whom God has chosen? It is God who justifies. Who then is the one who condemns? No one" (vv. 33–34). While Paul never shirked his responsibility to correct believers, he clearly rejects toxic shame. He teaches the Roman church to ignore condemnation and place no trust in it.

Condemnation is *satanically tainted shame* that must be rejected.

Our discipleship practices need to help us develop a real resistance to condemnation.[3] Condemnation will come at us, but we should learn to handle it like we would bad weather. We shelter ourselves.[4] Condemnation can get under our armor if we think, *Maybe this person is right. Maybe I am a bad person.* We are paying more attention to a toxic message than our true identity as God's children. We need to clean up messages from our past that Satan uses to contaminate our identities, and this may require healing trauma. See Further Resources for This Chapter for more on trauma.

When we confuse toxic and healthy corrections, we open ourselves to condemnation. Proverbs 15:31 says that those who heed correction become wise. If we mistake people's accusations for godly correction, we will not protect ourselves from condemnation. Knowing the difference between healthy shame and toxic shame gives us confidence to reject condemnation and accept healthy correction.

Narcissists use condemnation skillfully as a strategy for success. If your community has a narcissist in a position of influence, you must train yourself to reject his or her toxic shame. Condemnation should roll off of you like water off a duck's back. A firm rejection of condemnation also is a way of loving a narcissist. You are giving them a window into a life free of toxic shame. Who knows, maybe God will use you. Your refusal to accept condemnation may be their first step toward healing.

Healthy Correction

Like most of you, I have received both toxic and healthy correction. Although both provoke shame, they are worlds apart in how they feel in my body. When correction is delivered through a loving attachment (*hesed*) and the person is properly trained and mature, correction feels painful and loving at the same time. The corrector knows how to be careful with their use of shame. They are kind but firm. There is not a hint of condemnation or contempt; nor is there selfish ambition. I can see in their eyes that our relationship is secure.

If my community has developed a group identity around the importance of correction, I am in the right place to see my character formed. "We are the kind of people who eagerly accept correction, knowing that correction forms us into the image of Christ." My brain will latch onto the group identity and ask, *What do my people do when we forget to act like ourselves?*

Training people how to correct each other is risky. Narcissistic and selfishly ambitious people may try to follow the "steps to healthy correction," but they do not have the attachment and maturity. It may not be the moment to deliver correction. We must rely on God and never be in a hurry to help someone remember who they are. It can wait a day or two to make sure your own heart is lined up with Jesus' heart and timing.

Healthy correction is always an invitation to return to our true identity and start acting like ourselves again. We are reminding someone who forgot, "This is not you. You forgot who you are. Let me remind you who we are." I often ask for healthy correction from my wife when I realize that I'm not acting like myself. I don't have to wait around for her to notice. If your forgetful moment happens when no one is around, confess it later to someone you trust and let them remind you of your identity. This is Character Formation 101.

Jesus Giving Healthy Correction

Since Jesus designed the human body, including the brain, He understands how to help another person grow. Jesus gave us many examples of character formation during the three years He spent with His disciples. For example, in Luke 10, Jesus sends a group of His followers out into the surrounding towns to heal and tell everyone that the kingdom of God is near. The disciples returned with joy, saying, "Lord, even the demons submit to us in your name" (Luke 10:17). Most of us would not see this as an opportunity to correct their character, but Jesus does not hesitate. "He replied, 'I saw Satan fall like lightning from heaven. I have given you authority to trample on snakes and scorpions and to overcome all the power of the enemy; nothing will harm you. However, do not rejoice that the spirits submit to you, but rejoice that your names are written in heaven'" (vv. 18–20).

Note that Jesus did not spoil their joy. He validates their excitement, but He also notices a temptation, a potential bump down the road. He sees a deformation in their character. When we are doing the work of God's kingdom (and He is using us in powerful ways) it is tempting to be more excited about amazing results than about our *hesed* with God Himself. We become more excited about power than about knowing God. Jesus delivers correction in a way that speaks to us all. "However, do not rejoice that the spirits submit to you, but rejoice that your names are written in heaven" (Luke 10:20). First and foremost, we are the children of God, and our Father knows our names. We get our joy from His face shining on us, not from the fading glow of ministry success.

Jesus first affirms His relationship with His disciples by entering into their joy when they return. Rejoicing is the most easily forgotten step of discipleship. Healthy correction starts by affirming our *hesed* attachment and entering into the other person's emotional world. We never blindside people. When Jesus points out their character flaw, He quickly affirms their group identity: "We do not rejoice in our authority over spirits—or in our productivity, ministry growth, or fame. Instead, we are a people who rejoice that our Father knows our names. He identifies us as His own. That is the source of our joy."

This subtle correction shows that Jesus' radar is always on and looking for a chance to hone our character. The potential character flaws he detects would be overlooked by most of us. I can hear my own justifications if I were in Jesus' place. "Isn't it a small thing to worry about rejoicing too much over ministry success? Do they really need to be corrected? Shouldn't I just let them enjoy the moment?" I am skilled at inventing reasons to avoid correcting others. Jesus, on the other hand, had His radar on. He realized that the central work of God's kingdom is transforming character.

Later in the same chapter, we see His radar is still on. Jesus and His disciples are passing through a village, and a woman invites them to her home for dinner. As the woman and her sister prepare the meal, Jesus starts speaking. We are not told what He is saying, but His words stop one sister in her tracks. She did not want to miss a single word He said, so eventually she gave up any pretense of helping with the meal and sat down at Jesus' feet to listen.

The other sister is frantically planning the meal when she sees her sister just sitting there, doing nothing. Martha reacted the way many of us would react when preparing a last-minute un-planned meal. She walked up to Jesus and said, "Lord, don't you care that my sister has left me to do the work by myself? Tell her to help me!" His response is pure wisdom: "Martha, Martha," the Lord answered, "you are worried and upset about many things, but few things are needed—or indeed only one. Mary has chosen what is better, and it will not be taken away from her" (Luke 10:40–41).

Notice that Jesus starts by saying her name twice. Martha, Martha. Like the correction we studied above, Jesus is affirming His loving attachment to Martha. This is not an exasperated "Martha, Martha. What am I going to do with you?" Jesus is connecting to her. I believe He is looking her in the eyes. We can affirm our attachment to someone in many ways. In the previous story, Jesus validates the disciples' joy before correcting them. Here, Jesus simply says, "Martha, Martha." These two words combined with Jesus' loving gaze calm her down and prepare her heart.

I would not have corrected Martha if I were in the same situation. I would tell Mary to help her sister, and I would stop teaching until later, when everyone could listen. Whew! Problem solved. Conflict avoided! Unlike me, Jesus does not hesitate. He understands that character change is the central work of His kingdom. He also knows that He is correcting not just Martha. Everyone in the room, including you and me thousands of years later, is being formed by Jesus' admonition.

The specific correction Jesus delivers is blunt: "You are worried and upset about many things, but few things are needed—or indeed only one. Mary has chosen what is better, and it will not be taken away from her." This response is an echo of the group identity He formed in His Sermon on the Mount in Matthew 6:33: "But seek first his kingdom and his righteousness, and all these things will be given to you as well." We do not know whether Martha was present for that sermon, but His teaching had possibly spread by word of mouth to reach Martha. Jesus had previously prepared the soil with group identity. This is the progression:

Joy ➔ *Hesed* ➔ Group Identity ➔ Correction

We see Jesus intentionally forming group identity as a precursor to correcting character. This agrees with what brain science tells us regarding how our brains are structured to form character. Jesus has diligently prepared the relational soil to arrive at the place where His corrections will bring transformation. Jesus is the One who designed our brains and He knows how they work.

We have seen several examples of the Master correcting people as a part of His daily life. These examples flowed from Him naturally because His radar was on. He lived his life scanning His surroundings for opportunities to transform people's character. I will share some of my own attempts to keep my own radar on and some examples of others doing it well. We learn by hearing examples of both offering correction and also being on the receiving end. We will start with an incident that happened before I met Jim and had the benefit of his training. Let's look at three ways I could respond to a situation that happened with my son during his junior year of high school. (I have his permission to share this story.)

At the end of spring break, my son and a group of his friends had the brilliant idea to commit an act of vandalism on school property, hoping that it would add a few days of vacation to their spring break. Little permanent damage was done, but they all were caught and suspended. This was his junior year of high school, right as he was applying to colleges. Put yourself in my shoes, as his parent, and look at three possible responses I might have as a father:

Response #1: "*Son, that was a stupid thing to do! Now you have ruined your chances to go to college. What college is going to accept your application when they see that you tried to vandalize your school? What is wrong with you?*"

This response is a classic example of toxic shame. Unlike Jesus, I do not affirm the relationship, I say "you" without talking about "we," and I do not invite him back to his real identity. I leave him with no hope or path out. He is stuck in his failure and probably feels despair.

Response #2: *"Son, I did some stupid things when I was your age. Schools did not have security cameras, so I never got caught. You are not stupid, but you did a stupid thing. Now you have to pay for it, but I still love you. I will walk with you in this."*

This feels better because I do not leave him in toxic shame. I affirm our relationship and give him some hope. However, I do not specifically point out what he did wrong. I just call it "stupid," a general description that is not easily tied to group identity. More importantly, I do not appeal to who we are. I leave group identity out of the equation, so the circuits of my son's brain that Jesus designed to form his character do not come into play.

Response #3: I put both of my hands on his shoulders and look at him in the eyes for a few seconds. I communicate nonverbally that this is really hard but we are with him. Then I say, *"Elias, I did a lot of stupid things when I was your age. I didn't get caught, but honestly, I'm glad you got caught. This is a great chance for you to grow, because you forgot who you are. Allow me to remind you. We do not destroy the property of others just because we want a few more days of vacation or to prove something to our friends. Instead, we are a family who values the property of others, even school property. You stopped acting like yourself, and this is going to cost you. This will be hard, but your mom and I will walk through this with you."*

This is an example of using healthy shame to correct the character of a young man who did something foolish. I affirm our relationship both nonverbally and verbally. I remind him who we are and invite him back into his identity. I talk about his failure specifically enough so that our group identity can correct him. I don't leave him alone, but I also am not too nice. I let him feel a prick of shame. That's all he needs to change.

Self-Justification

Let's talk about being on the receiving end of correction. The main barrier we have to being formed by healthy correction is self-justification. When a person responds to correction by trying to justify themselves, the Bible calls this "stiff-necked." Instead of receiving correction, they respond by trying to win the argument. Underneath this, they are really trying to avoid shame.

We see a clear picture of self-justification in the life of King Saul. On one occasion, he had clear instructions to wait for the prophet Samuel before engaging in a battle. He needed Samuel to seek God's direction for the king, but Samuel does not arrive on time. Saul gets impatient and takes matters into his own hands.

> Saul's men began to scatter. So he said, "Bring me the burnt offering and the fellowship offerings." And Saul offered up the burnt offering. Just as he finished making the offering, Samuel arrived, and Saul went out to greet him.
>
> "What have you done?" asked Samuel.
>
> Saul replied, "When I saw that the men were scattering, and that you did not come at the set time, and that the Philistines were assembling at Mikmash, I thought, 'Now the Philistines will come down against me at Gilgal, and I have not sought the LORD's favor.' So I felt compelled to offer the burnt offering." (1 Sam. 13:8–12)

Saul's version of self-justification was that his men were scattering, and Samuel did not arrive on time. It was Samuel's fault that Saul had to offer up the burnt offerings because he did not arrive on time. Saul is trying to prove that he is innocent. He wants to come out the winner. Saul's justification eerily sounds like the excuse Adam offered God in the garden of Eden when he sinned.

"The woman you put here with me—she gave me some fruit from the tree, and I ate it" (Gen. 3:12). It was God's fault that he ate the forbidden fruit. God will never accept our self-justification because we are speaking the language of the serpent. Instead, God invites us to humble ourselves, abandon our self-justifications, and return to Him.

Our community must have well-formed identity so that self-justification does not take root in our interactions. In our basement

We are a people who really cannot stand self-justification and will not listen to it.

meetings, our group repeated this identity statement to each other: "We are a people who really cannot stand self-justification and will not listen to it."

When I justify myself, I erect a shield against any corrections that might be brought against me. My character will be impervious to change. We are most tempted to justify ourselves when another person is justifying herself or himself. When they want to win the argument, we must refuse to play this game. We do not try to win the "best self-justifier" trophy. Instead, we compete for "fastest to humble myself" trophy.

The Need for Training

None of what I have written about correction is cutting-edge Christian theology. Most of us have read Proverbs and have heard Solomon's teaching. Here is a taste:

> Whoever heeds life-giving correction
> will be at home among the wise. (15:31)

Those who disregard discipline despise themselves,
    but the one who heeds correction gains understand-
    ing. (15:32)

This next one wins the contest for bluntness:

Whoever loves discipline loves knowledge,
    but whoever hates correction is stupid. (12:1)

These are not difficult Scriptures to understand. Why, then, do we not see more transformational correction in our churches? One reason we fail to correct each other is because we reject all shame as bad. Correction might produce shame, so we keep our mouths shut. We may have seen correction that uses only toxic shame. We may be conflict avoiders or, as this chapter title suggests, maybe we are too nice.

If our churches are lacking the other soil components (joy, *hesed*, and group identity), correction will be less fruitful. Therefore, we might conclude that correction does not work.

All of these excuses point to the need for good teaching and training in our churches. We do not know how to correct each other in a way that is healthy because no one has trained us to do it.

A church that takes the Great Commission seriously intentionally trains its people to give and receive loving correction. The leaders and mature Christians are diligent to model a life of constant healthy correction. A mature disciple of Jesus is eager to accept correction and share stories of being corrected, and we make sure this becomes part of the relational DNA of our community. Consider the following example of a mature Christian leading the way:

I arrived in Mexico City to help facilitate a weekend retreat with my friend James Henderson, who lives in Mexico. He picked me up from the airport, and we were excited to be together and work side by side at the retreat. We see each other only several times a year, so our car rides back to his house are always filled with updating each other on our lives.

"Michel," James started the conversation, "I have to share something with you that I'm ashamed happened yesterday. Mateo called me and asked whether I had sent him the materials for the retreat. I realized I had completely forgotten, and I said, 'Yes, Mateo, they are on the way,' thinking that I would do it as soon as I hung up. Then it hit me what I had done. I lied to him! I lied to my good friend! I immediately called him back and said, 'Mateo, I just lied to you. I'm so busy that I forgot, and instead of owning up to it, I tried to be sneaky. I lied to you, and I ask for your forgiveness.'"

James is a mature man. The first thing he wanted me to know about his life was not the latest success story of his ministry. He wanted to share with me that he had lied. He also demonstrated how to handle shame in a relational way. His instinct might have been to make excuses or hide. Instead, James called Mateo and connected to him during his shame. The people of our churches need to see and hear healthy examples of handling shame in a relational way to correct flaws in our character. (See Resources at the end of the chapter).[5] This is quickly becoming a lost skill in many churches, and people like James are needed to train the next generation.

In chapter 4, we discovered that sharing weakness increases *hesed*, one of the four ingredients of healthy soil. By sharing our stories of being corrected, we are adding two ingredients to our relational soil at once. When I share my character flaws, I am sharing a weakness, which increases our *hesed*. At the same time, I am giving you an example of eagerly accepting correction. Two essential nutrients at the same time! Our relational soil is rapidly improving.

We not only need to share stories of giving and receiving correction. We also need lots of practice. *Training* is another word for repetition. We need reps. This is a big hole in our Christian practices that results in poor soil. If we want transformational soil, we need to train our people.

We did lots of reps in the training group that met in our basement every week. Here is an example of a correction exercise we repeated, using a different message each time:

"In groups of about five people create a healthy shame message for me when I am *ignoring the feelings of others.*"

Note: A healthy shame message states "we do not" and then states who we are with a Christlike character response.

"We do not _____. Instead, we are a people who _____."[6]

We did this exercise for a different character flaw each week. Later in the training, we practiced correcting each other with real-life flaws. It was awkward at times. Like most training, after doing reps, we improved and it came more naturally.

The formula above, "We do not _____. Instead, we are a people who _____," is like training wheels to help us learn. Once we get comfortable with the essence of healthy correction, we no longer need the training wheels. We can naturally blend the elements of healthy correction into a conversation. My wife and I saw the training bleed into our daily lives. Let me share an example. We were cooking together one night when my wife surprised me by her question, "Are you in a state of mind to receive correction?"

I felt a knot form in my stomach, and I thought, "Oh no, what did I do?" Then my training kicked in. I thought of group identity.

"We are a people who eagerly accept correction, knowing that correction transforms our character into the image of Christ." The knot loosened, and I said, "Yes. Give it to me."

Claudia then reminded me of something I did. Several days earlier at the supermarket, there was a man at a booth selling gourmet salad dressings. He had us try each one, all of which were delicious. I glanced at the expensive price and turned to my wife and said, "I bet you could figure out how to make this dressing at home. We have all of the ingredients."

The man's face fell. It all happened so fast and was subtle and nonverbal. As soon as she mentioned this encounter, I felt ashamed.

Claudia looked at me and reminded me, "That man was proud of his new company and the quality of his products. Whether or not you desire to buy the dressing, you devalued his work in front of his face. We are not a people who devalue the work of others. Instead, we always look for ways to affirm the value of people."

I felt ashamed, but my wife's eyes clearly stated that she loved me, even when I do not act like myself. This correction was not damaging our *hesed*. Rather, she was loving me by correcting me. She refused to be nice. Instead, she was kind and loving. After my initial fearful reaction, I eagerly accepted her correction.

During our training with Jim, he commented that as we get accustomed to the benefits of healthy correction, we will be excited when someone corrects us. Our first thought will be, "Oh boy! What am I going to learn about myself that will make me more like Jesus?" This attitude was foreign to me and seemed impossible when I first heard it. I had an automatic defensive reaction to being corrected. As we practiced, my instant reaction to correction changed from self-protection to guarded excitement. Good soil and intentional training were bearing fruit. I needed reps.

In churches, we not only need to teach healthy correction,

we also need to train our people to reject condemnation, the unhealthy form of correction. When someone uses toxic shame to correct another person, the correction not only fails to touch their character, but also causes harm. We see toxic correction when pastors use guilt to motivate people. You will get a chance to practice rejecting condemnation in the exercises at the end of this chapter.

We will see in the next chapter that narcissists use toxic shame as their strategy to win. Training our people to reject toxic shame creates a narcissism-resistant community. The narcissist's weapon—toxic shame—is ineffective in healthy soil.

- -

When we in the church fail to teach and model healthy correction, we see little character transformation. A high-joy, high-*hesed* community with a well-developed group identity is ready to flourish, but it still lacks an essential nutrient. By training our people to correct each other through affirming our *hesed* and group identity, we grow what we were meant to grow—Christlike character. We refuse to be too nice. Instead, our correction is a loving affirmation to shine the character of Jesus more fully.

- -

GROUP DISCUSSION QUESTIONS

1. Complete the Soil Sample 4: "Culture of Correction" Assessment in Appendix A for your Christian community. Discuss the strength of your community's "culture of correction."

2. Read Philippians 4:2–3 and notice how Paul corrects two women.
   a. How does he affirm their *hesed*?
   b. How does Paul correct these women?
   c. Why do you think he mentions the book of life?
3. Read 1 Thessalonians 4:3–8. What is the healthy shame message here? Restate it in your own words: We do not _____. Instead, we are a people who _____.
4. Read the story of Martha and Mary in Luke 10:38–42. Restate Jesus' correction of Martha as a general statement of how God's children act: We are a people who _____.

TRY IT OUT

Come up with a healthy shame message for the following two scenarios. Follow the format: "We do not _____. Instead, we are a people who _____."

1. Joe and his wife are having an intense conversation about a financial problem. In the middle of the conversation, a salesman knocks on the door and tries to sell Joe a magazine subscription. Joe said, "I don't have time for this," and shut the door in his face.
   a. What is Joe's character flaw?
   b. What is a group identity statement that shows Joe how we act here?
   c. Create a healthy shame message for Joe. (Use the formula above.)
   d. Now, instead of just filling in the blanks in the formula, have a conversation with Joe, using someone in the group to play him. Practice working in the healthy shame message as a natural part of our conversation to help

correct Joe's character flaw. Be sure to affirm the relationship, but don't avoid shame.

2. It is Halloween, and your kids are out trick-or-treating When they come home with their bags full of candy, you hear one child say to another, "The Smiths were not home tonight, so they put out a bowl of candy with a sign that said, 'Take one, please.' We poured the entire bowl into our bags."

   a. What is your child's character flaw?

   b. What is a group identity statement that shows the child how we act here?

   c. Create a healthy shame message for your child. (Use the formula above.)

   d. Now, instead of just filling in the blanks in the formula, have a conversation with your child, using someone in the group to play him or her. Practice working in the healthy shame message as a natural part of the conversation to help correct their character flaw. Be sure to affirm the relationship but don't avoid shame.

3. Rejecting condemnation exercise: In your group come up with a list of about five common condemnations you hear. Pass the list around the circle, one by one.

   a. Have each person look at the list and pick one of the condemnation statements, and have the person on the left read it out loud to you as though they were condemning you.

   b. You and the rest of the group respond in unison by saying, "There is no condemnation in Christ Jesus."

   c. Go around until everyone has had a chance to reject condemnation.

FURTHER RESOURCES FOR THIS CHAPTER

Narcissism:
- E. James Wilder, *The Pandora Problem*

Shame:
- Curt Thompson, *The Soul of Shame*

Practicing Healthy Shame:
- E. James Wilder, *The Pandora Problem*
- Barbara Moon, *The Pandora Problem Companion Guide*

7

....

Narcissism: The Relational Infection

Land that drinks in the rain often falling on it and that produces a crop useful to those for whom it is farmed receives the blessing of God. But land that produces thorns and thistles is worthless and is in danger of being cursed. In the end it will be burned.

Hebrews 6:7–8

MANY YEARS AGO, I caught an eye infection that resisted being cured. My eyes would turn red and become swollen. Antibiotic drops would knock the infection down for a while, but a few weeks later it would return. After several months of this, my ophthalmologist said, "I think what we have here is a cultural problem." He explained that my eyes had a culture that was conducive to growing bacteria. I had never thought of my eyes having a culture, but I followed his instructions to change the culture of my eyes through washing and warm compresses. I admit I was skeptical, but eventually the infections disappeared and haven't returned. I changed the culture of my eyes.

The church has both a culture and an infection. Even if there were a magical antibiotic, the infection would keep recurring until the culture changes. The culture of a church is its relational soil, and the infection thrives in depleted soil. A chain of events has left us with exhausted soil that bears little fruit. Unfortunately, the bad news gets worse. The depleted soil of half-brained Christianity not only chokes spiritual formation, it also creates a culture where a certain relational infection thrives, spreads, and returns.

Relationally impoverished soil leaves a community vulnerable to the spread of narcissism, especially in positions of leadership and influence. Enriching the soil is the only long-term solution. We can remove narcissists from their positions of influence, but without adding the essential soil nutrients, the infection will return. The consequences of this disease devastate churches and families.

The Disease

It surprised me how often the topic of narcissism arose during our meetings. The training was focused on growing our character, but when Jim Wilder first talked about the relational infection in the church, you could hear a pin drop in the room. Most of us had been involved in churches and ministries for a long time. We all had bumped up against the infection that Jim was explaining. We had seen leaders act in ways that troubled us. Some of us had kept quiet. Others spoke up. Some of us were fired for speaking up. We knew something was wrong but did not have an explanation for it. We had no label for it.

After the meeting, we talked outside, lingering for over an hour. One friend shared his experience with me. He was the high-school pastor of a well-established church and worked under a beloved pastor. During a planning meeting with the leadership team, Dave disagreed with one of the pastor's ideas and explained why. Later that afternoon, he noticed a piece of paper had been slipped under his office door. The beloved pastor wrote him a note: "Never disagree with me in front of the elders again!" Stories like this kept popping up after our meetings.

Quite a few churches were represented in our group. We heard suspicions, particularly from the millennial generation, that something was wrong with the way people were being treated. Jim shared his concern that narcissism was becoming a normal and accepted behavior in Christian churches and families. We see a narcissist and think, *There is a strong leader.* Exactly the opposite is true. We are intentionally selecting leaders with narcissistic tendencies because we have a broken picture of healthy leadership.

I have always been confused about the definition of narcissism. The common understanding is that narcissists are self-centered and grandiose. The diagnostic definition avoids a hard category of "narcissist" but provides a sliding scale for severity and a list of characteristics. People with narcissism lack empathy, have a strong need for admiration, and want to be the biggest personality in the room.

I was sufficiently confused, so I asked Jim for a definition from the perspective of brain science. He explained that a narcissist *is someone who is unable to metabolize shame in a relational way.* Whoa! That was not the answer I expected. Metabolize shame? What does that mean?

Narcissism and Shame

We learned that our brains are designed to metabolize emotions. Shame is one of the six big emotions with dedicated neurological circuitry (that is, sadness, anger, fear, shame, hopeless despair, disgust). In the healthy case, shame gets digested through relational attachments—through *hesed*. We studied this concept in the previous chapter when we saw that the first step in correcting another person's character is affirming our relationship. For example, if you see me do something that does not reflect the character of Jesus, you have a chance to change my character. This growth opportunity involves helping me metabolize the shame of my flaw.

You approach me at the proper time and say, "Michel, I really enjoy our friendship and care about you. I sense that you forgot who you were back there. Are you open to being reminded of who we are?"

I feel ashamed, and, in the healthy case, I sense our attachment and receive your message. The shame gets digested quickly and is displaced by peace and relief. If the correction is done properly and I am humble and receptive, you have helped mold my character. I am now a little more like Jesus thanks to you. In God's kingdom, shame is always combined with a strong dose of love.

However, we can also metabolize shame in nonrelational ways, and this corrupted digestion is the playground of narcissism. We view narcissism in this book in terms of character, not as a technical psychological classification. When we speak of narcissists, we are talking about people who have narcissistic traits that dominate their character. Narcissists have formed unhealthy character habits for interacting with others.

For example, if I am infected with this relational disease, I will respond differently to your loving attempts to remind me of who I am. I will see our interaction as a threat. Our conversation becomes an argument that I must win. My motivation to defeat you is especially fierce if you are correcting my character and my leadership. I think, *This person, who is trying to make me look bad, must lose!*

We will have difficulty improving our character if we refuse to accept healthy correction. In the previous chapter, we read

Proverbs 15:31: "Whoever heeds life-giving correction will be at home among the wise." When we ignore this path to wisdom—by refusing to learn and grow from the people around us—we are heading toward narcissism. We cannot handle the shame of being reproved, and we do not want to learn because we are focused on winning. In this state, our character is immovable.

Narcissists will not accept a healthy reminder when their character is flawed, but they are skilled in using toxic shame against others. In the previous chapter we emphasized the importance of refusing to accept toxic shame, and this is especially crucial in the presence of a narcissist. If we are weak and untrained, the narcissist will make us think we are crazy, because they are masters of wielding condemnation.[1]

Communities with rich soil train their people to protect themselves from toxic shame, and this renders powerless one of the narcissist's favorite weapons. Our example gives the narcissist hope. They see you acting in a way that seems impossible to them. You are refusing to accept condemnation, and you are also accepting the healthy shame of correction. You have given the narcissistic brain an image that creates a new option for behavior. Remember that we change through imitation. It is impossible to teach a narcissist new behavior. They must see you metabolize shame with their own eyes.

- -

EXAMPLES OF TOXIC SHAME VS. HEALTHY SHAME

Toxic: You are so passive-aggressive!

Healthy: If you have a complaint against me, I'm fine with that. Bring it to me directly instead of talking to others. I'm the only one who can change me.

Toxic: I'm not going to let you go rogue in your ministry!

Healthy: We need to ensure that what you are doing is coherent with the direction of our church. You might have some great ideas, so let's keep in close communication on this.

Toxic: Who are you to criticize me?

Healthy: Your criticism hurts, but I want to be open to learning from it. Tell me more.

- -

Nonrelational strategies to digest shame by winning seem necessary to us when we are convinced that all shame is toxic. When we do not know how to deal with shame in a relational way, we create complex strategies to avoid it at all costs. These anti-shame strategies drive much of the behavior that we see listed in popular and psychological explanations of narcissism. These strategies are not the disease itself but the symptoms. At its core, narcissism is a shame disease.[2]

The Narcissistic Pastor

Unfortunately, the narcissistic "I must win" strategy can spill over into Christian communities, which explains why we see narcissistic behavior in leaders of organizations and churches. They manage shame by winning instead of metabolizing shame through *hesed* relationships. That is why people with narcissistic tendencies seek to be the CEO, the head pastor, the lead elder, or the hidden influencer. It's important to note that not all of these positions are filled by narcissists, but people who grapple with narcissism do crave these positions of influence because they feed their sense of being special. Once they get their hands on the power they crave, they will not want to release it. You will see these positions turn into lifetime appointments until the people around these leaders wise up.

When a Christian community has low joy, weak *hesed*, and a poorly developed group identity, the culture is armed for narcissism to spread. If we eliminate the immediate infection, it soon returns. Without strong attachments and relational skills, narcissism flourishes—especially in leadership.

You do not have to look hard to see examples of the destruction left by narcissism. While paying more attention to this over the years and even more acutely while writing and researching this book, I have been saving articles on church-fueled narcissism gone very bad. I have a long list, but here are a few pieces:

- The sexually inappropriate behavior of a pastor is exposed, but not by the elder team. They refused to believe accusations. The pastor denies all allegations, even in the face of overwhelming evidence.
- The leader of a large Christian organization is observed labeling constituents with pejorative names. An employee describes the work environment as being based on fear. The leadership denies all charges.
- A lead minister is accused of financial mismanagement, deception, and bullying. The elder board supports him until irrefutable evidence confirms the claims.
- The pastor of a large church resigns after being accused of having sexual encounters with multiple teenage girls in a previous job. He is accused of using his position of authority to take advantage of his victims. When parents confront the church's leadership about the alleged abuse of authority, they are urged to keep things quiet.

I could continue with more examples and make this a very long chapter, but I think you get the idea. We are not implying a clinical diagnosis of narcissism here. But these present examples of classic narcissistic character on display. Frequently, the stories feature common threads running through these organizations: a rubber stamp board, a personality-driven organization, and poor financial accountability. These issues, and others, need to be addressed, but there is usually no mention of what is going on underneath the visible behavior. What is happening in the hearts of these leaders and in the hearts of the people who surround them?[3] We must address the relational soil that nourishes and encourages narcissistic behavior, otherwise the church will often select a narcissistic pastor to fill the position of the recently fired narcissist. Or another narcissistic leader will emerge from the staff of the church and finally get the leadership position they felt they always deserved. The infection returns.

The perpetrators in these negative headlines suffer from the effects of half-brained Christianity like the rest of us. More significantly, they did not do the hard work of character formation and developing relational skills that would have extracted their narcissistic tendencies and replaced them with the beautiful character of Christ. They are logical consequences of the great omission. When we fail to form character in churches, we end up having leaders with poorly formed character—pastors who do not act like Jesus.

How does narcissism play out in the life of a pastor? An inability to metabolize shame inflates a person's need to be special, a narcissistic strategy of handling shame. Wanting to be special is a healthy desire we all have, a God-given desire. However, narcissists are unable to satisfy this need relationally, so they are driven to perform and succeed. We see this as good leadership. Narcissists satisfy their need to be special through performance and winning, using Christian ministry as the vehicle.

Infected leaders use ministry to communicate, "I'm not just special, I'm more special than all of you." Their ability to win helps them avoid shame, their greatest fear. But as we have seen, without shame, our character does not change. Giftedness, ministry success, and bold leadership may look good on the surface, but the inner motivation has been detached from relationships. We may find this confusing, because their ministries look impressive.

The apostle John wrote about such a leader who was intent on winning. He warns his readers about a certain man, Diotrephes. "I wrote to the church, but Diotrephes, who loves to be first, will not welcome us" (3 John 9). Diotrephes was a winner.

Paul warns, "I know that after my departure fierce wolves will come in among you, not sparing the flock" (Acts 20:29 ESV). The need to be first leads to an abandonment of Christlike character.

A manifestation of "I must win" leadership is a love of measurability and numbers. These leaders love motivating people by growth and numbers and put them on display as proof that "we are winning." True discipleship gets ignored under their leadership because they have little time for activities that are hard to measure and display. That's not to say that they don't talk about discipleship and spiritual formation, especially in front of a crowd. They talk about discipleship to prove that they are serious about obeying Jesus, but they rarely if ever do it. The actual hard work of discipleship is neglected. Subordinates who advocate for the slow, messy work of discipleship will soon find themselves looking for a new job. They are promoting a priority that the narcissist finds unimportant.

Narcissistic leaders love a good cause, and their cause may be truly important—fighting corruption, protecting the poor, reaching university students for Christ, defending good doctrine, spreading the gospel, or planting churches in prisons. The cause is presented to the community as the narcissist's own grand vision, and it becomes so important that ministry is elevated above relationships rather than flowing from relationships. Let me state this again, because it gets to the center of the dysfunction: *Ministry becomes more important than relationships.* Now we are finally looking at the soil and not just the symptoms, and a soil analysis reveals depleted *hesed.*

If anyone gets in the way of the *great cause*, they get sacrificed on the altar of the leader's vision. These bold leaders get results. When they don't get results, they create a narrative that lays the fault at someone else's feet. Narcissists are good at using others' weaknesses against them while keeping their own character insulated and untouchable. They are happy to sacrifice other people because doing so feeds their sense of greatness and their ability to make tough choices—all characteristics of a "courageous leader."

Most narcissists envision themselves as great leaders. They like being the biggest personality in the room, the one in charge. They are surrounded by people who extol their giftedness and vision. It is common to hear this pastor tout his own leadership skills, and the validating bubble community surrounding him agrees. "He is such a visionary!" "He is such a courageous leader!" This language is foreign to the kingdom of God.

We often see an affirming bubble group surrounding a narcissistic leader. Instead of giving firm and gentle feedback, the group justifies and enables the flaws in the leader's character. If a person dares to push back, she is quickly pushed out. Narcissists are skilled at creating narratives, so the explanation for her leaving staff will seem quite reasonable: "She does not align with our vision, so we all agreed that it was time to transition her out." The true reason for her departure was that she was trying to pop the bubble and correct the leader's character.

A narcissist may accept correction on a peripheral issue from time to time, to be able to say, "Look! I'm humble. I accept criticism," but not on a central character issue. When confronted with a flaw in their character—and especially their leadership—they will massage it and redefine it until it is peripheral. They are very tricky here because they are protecting their specialness.

The pulpit is a strong magnet for narcissists, and they use it to achieve what they crave: attention, control, being at the center, being able to create the narrative. For the narcissist pastor, the sermon becomes performance art. The overemphasis on the sermon in modern Christianity is like chumming the water for narcissists. Up on a stage, the grand leader can appear to have a strong connection with the congregation while maintaining real relational distance. The stage, the image magnification, and the microphone allow pastors to appear close while avoiding real attachments to anyone who might threaten their control and sense of being special. From this exalted position they can choose their friends carefully. Surrounded by a supportive community of weakly attached people with a shallow group identity, pastors can exercise significant control.

Some scholars are attempting to measure the prevalence of narcissism in Christian leadership, but have yet to agree on the proper measurement instruments.[4] We will have to wait for new studies before we can quantify the extent and depth of narcissism in the pastorate. For now we can look at the prevalence of narcissism in terms of behavior. If we suspect that our Christian communities are under narcissistic influence, we expect to see certain behavioral patterns:

- A lack of concern when causing pain in others
- An emphasis on the bold visionary leadership of the pastor
- An "us versus them" mentality
- The creation of narratives that support the leader's view of

reality, even if the facts get massaged to fit this view
- Harsh and abrupt firings of subordinates; firings with little explanation or communication
- A submissive elder board that is obstructed from true input and feedback
- A church staff that sees its job as submissively implementing the leader's grand vision
- The leader's vision for the church is emphasized more than Christ's vision for the church
- A culture where submissive obedience to the leader is more important than character and maturity
- A church staff environment where the leader is seldom given feedback or critique, but where the leader readily and openly criticizes others
- Churches where the image and personality of the leader is inflated and projected to a size that overshadows Christ
- A church that hires a leader by looking intently at the candidate's giftedness and ability while only glancing superficially, if at all, at character and maturity
- A leader who gets away with all sorts of behaviors that would result in the immediate firing of a subordinate
- Elders and staff that say, "How could we ever get rid of him?" or, "The church would fall apart without her"
- A leader who cares more about being right and winning than being good and loving
- A leader who will turn another person from "friend" to "excluded" in an instant
- A leader who has the ability to cut off a friendship and move on to other friends while feeling very little pain

Certain people might have come to your mind as you read the list. If you are like me, you see some of your own weaknesses there, too. These traits reveal character that starkly contrasts what we see in Jesus, the perfect leader. What is missing is a stable and growing Christlike character and healthy soil, especially *hesed*.

Self-Justification

Another characteristic of narcissism deserves our attention. How do I respond to correction? Much is revealed by our answer to this question. Do I humble myself and listen, or do I try to justify myself? Do I humbly bow my head or do I stiffen my neck? We seldom hear teaching about self-justification in our churches. If we are honest, few of us enjoy someone criticizing our character. If I have narcissistic tendencies, my reaction to your feedback will be to stiffen my neck against your correction and justify myself. I will show you that I am right and you are wrong. If I think all shame is toxic, I will interpret your admonition to mean that I am not special. Self-justification is the first weapon I reach for to defend myself.

Self-justification can be deceiving. We choose narcissists for our leaders precisely because they are so good at justifying themselves. They are good at having all the answers and sounding right. People who have not been trained to spot self-justification misjudge it for self-confidence. To the discerning, the justifications sound reasonable at first, but they know something is wrong below the surface. A stiff neck is often well hidden.

In the previous chapter we saw that Samuel offered King Saul a life-giving rebuke, but the king used self-justification to swat it away. His specialness was threatened when Samuel pointed out his flawed character. Saul was so desperate that he blamed the prophet for his own disobedience. He reflexively reached for his trustiest weapon: self-justification.

Like yawning, self-justification is contagious. If you and I are arguing, and I justify myself, your reflex will be to justify yourself in response. Remember what we learned about changing our automatic (preconscious) responses through group identity in chapter 5. We need a group identity that says, "We are a people who really cannot stand self-justification and will not listen to it." God is our defender, so we do not need to justify ourselves. We must train ourselves to resist justifying. When we follow Saul's example, it never ends well.

We practiced recognizing and withstanding self-justification every week in our basement. We built up our ability to detect self-justification in ourselves and others. I had never been trained to spot and eliminate self-justification, but I quickly understood the benefits of this exercise. Because of our practice, I feel that I spot justification quickly.

- -

EXAMPLES OF SELF-JUSTIFICATION

- I don't need to pray about it; I know what God is going to say
- We should just forgive and overlook it
- I'm not justifying myself; you are
- You are way out of line, rebelling against God's authority, and should not speak to me that way
- We all have to make sacrifices for this vision to become reality
- I cannot believe the stupidity of what you are doing
- You wouldn't understand it in a million years
- Do I have to tell you again? (with contempt)
- You should forgive and forget
- God put me in charge here

Taken from *The Pandora Problem*[5]

- -

One week, Jim gave us the following example of self-justification:

> Someone says to you, "You wouldn't understand in a million years."

Does that look like a self-justification to you? It did not to me when I first heard it. Then I reflected on my years working in the tech industry. One senior coworker came to mind who had more experience than the rest of us on the team. We would occasionally need to ask him questions about our project. He had a reputation. If he had to explain something more than once, he would become angry and insulting. While he did not say it verbally, the look on his face communicated, "If I have to explain something to you twice, you won't understand it in a million years."

In the training, we made a list of weaknesses that hide behind this self-justification. Self-justification is a weakness that masquerades as a strength. We should be able to find hidden weaknesses if we look hard enough. Identifying the cracks in defensive statements help us see them from God's perspective. We were training ourselves to no longer be fooled.

It seemed like once we spotted the first weakness, we started seeing many of them. We came up with the following weaknesses of the self-justification listed above:

- This statement is belittling and impatient
- It shuts down further discussion
- It keeps the self-justifier from needing to explain further
- This justification shows arrogance: "I'm so much smarter than you that you will never understand my lofty thinking"
- This statement might also be a cover-up for laziness

THE OTHER HALF OF CHURCH
THE OTHER HALF OF CHURCH

Self-justification is a weakness that masquerades as a strength.

Then Jim asked what can we do to ensure these weaknesses do not take root in our community. We talked about how our group can become a place where, when a person says, "You wouldn't understand in a million years!" we would instantly spot this as self-justification and know how to help the person act in accordance with their true identity. First, we created a group identity statement that would become part of our common understanding:

We are a people who patiently teach and help people, even when they struggle to understand, because this is how God treats us.

Another idea was to share a story of when we were impatient with a struggling learner and how we realized that we were wrong. I remembered one time when my young daughter spilled something and made a big mess. I overreacted and she looked at me and said, "But it's okay. It's not a big deal." She stopped me in my tracks because she was right and I was wrong to overreact. Stories give the self-justifier mental pictures of what Christ's character looks like in this situation.

- -

FACING SELF-JUSTIFIED PEOPLE

- This task is for a community with mature leaders
- Demonstrate humble character
- Don't try to prove we are right

- Avoid all condemnation
  + Don't receive condemnation
- Develop excellent judgment
- Recognize, avoid, and address Christian forms of
  self-justification
  + "I have faith"
  + "You cannot judge me"
- When the group has been impacted, correct the self-justification in front of the group. Keep our *hesed* clean
  + Don't hold grudges or seek revenge
  + Keep compassion high
  + Our goal is discipleship, not a one-time correction
- See things God's way
  + Observe first
  + Dialogue about observations with God in our identity group
  + Notice all self-justification
  + Notice all condemnation
  + Notice humble character
  + Make wise judgments

Taken from *The Pandora Problem*, 183

Enemy Mode: Your Brain on Narcissism

God designed a complex network of neurological circuits to work together to help us stay relationally connected and attuned to each other. When these relational circuits are running as designed, we call this "Relational Mode." Our emotional and relational sensitivity is working and we look at life through a relational filter. We are emotionally attuned to other people and share their pain. In this mode our identity is stable and we spread joy and life to those around us.

A surprising feature is that relational circuits can operate kind of like a circuit breaker. When we use too many electrical appliances at the same time in our kitchen, this will cause our breaker switch to pop. The electricity stays off until I find the breaker in our breaker panel and flip it back on. Similarly, in emotionally intense situations, my emotional breaker can pop. My relational circuits dim or go off entirely. Suddenly, I have difficulty feeling my connections to those around me. Relationships are no longer my first priority. I am focused on stopping pain and solving problems. I am no longer processing life through the lens of relationships.

When our circuits go off, we lose our sense of connection to people. We have difficulty sensing God's presence, too, and we even lose our sense of connection with our bodies. This brain state is called "Enemy Mode," because people start to feel like enemies to be defeated or problems to be solved. Most of the time, these "enemies" are people we usually like but, at that moment, don't seem to be on our side. I might even snap at my mother if she steps on my toe.

One of the first skills we learn in full-brained discipleship is to detect when our relational circuits have shut off and learn how to turn them back on. Before doing anything else, and especially before doing something that is relationally challenging—such as resolving a conflict—we need to first revive our relational circuits. The first step in any spiritual exercise must be to inspect our relational circuits and ensure they are on.[6] Our spiritual practices will be ineffective when these circuits are not working. Transformation depends on our relational circuits running smoothly.

You might be thinking, *I know where he is going with this. When people slip into narcissism, their relational circuits have turned off.*

They are in Enemy Mode. That is why they trample people. I would have said the same, but Enemy Mode is more nuanced. There are two types of Enemy Mode: Simple Enemy Mode and Predatory Enemy Mode.

In Simple Enemy Mode, all our relational circuits have shut down and we want people and problems to go away. We do not listen well to others, and our minds are locked on to our problems. We want to get away from a person, even if we love the person. In conflict, we will argue aggressively and will be quick to judge. We all lapse into Simple Enemy Mode from time to time.

In Predatory Enemy Mode, the circuits that govern our attachments (*hesed*) are turned off, so we do not treat weakness gently and have shallow bonds with people. Unlike Simple Enemy Mode, the rest of the relational circuits are on, but they are used for predatory advantage. This is the crafty nuance of Predatory Enemy Mode. We attune to others, not to show compassion but to exploit their weakness. We track the emotions of others in order to pounce.

When acting like predators, we hijack the circuits that notice weakness in others, and use them for a purpose God did not intend. He designed these circuits to help us show compassion for weakness and treat others gently—to act like protectors. In Predatory Enemy Mode, we use these circuits to stalk prey.

As you might have guessed, the narcissist brain operates in Predatory Enemy Mode. A relational person notices weakness in others and feels compassion, but narcissists devour the weak. When we advance ourselves by tracking the weaknesses of those around us, we are operating in Predatory Enemy Mode. We quickly divide people into "us versus them," and the "them" are used as stepping stones. A person working under the authority of a narcissist may go from "one of us" to "one of them" in an instant.

People in this predatory state evaluate others in the light of questions like: "How can I use this person to my advantage? What can they do for me? Do they love me enough, or should I get rid of them?"

A community that is ignorant of Enemy Mode is vulnerable to narcissistic influences. Members of that community may see Enemy Mode as strong leadership: "He may ruffle some feathers but he gets things done." A person in Enemy Mode is not walking in the character of Jesus.

We get our brains out of Simple Enemy Mode by quieting ourselves and talking to God about our emotions. We get out of Predatory Enemy Mode by sharing our opponent's emotional pain and praying for them. In our full-brain training, we practiced noticing Enemy Mode and getting quickly back to Relational Mode (see Appendix D). One tool for getting out of Enemy Mode is to give someone close to you permission to tell you when they see you in Enemy Mode. Another tool is to practice the Joy on Demand exercise in Appendix B. These and other tools can be learned but require considerable practice to be useful.[7]

If my enemy is a narcissist, I will still treat weakness tenderly, even though he or she may not treat me tenderly. Tenderness requires stable maturity and training. In order to love my enemy, I must have sufficient joy and love so it overflows to others. I must know who I am, because a narcissist will use condemnation to corrupt my identity. I will not fall for that deception if my group identity is well-developed and I'm trained to reject condemnation.

Now you understand why our relational soil is so important.

Loving my enemy does not mean giving someone a free pass. It is time for a corrective shame message. If I am growing in good soil, my joy, *hesed*, and group identity can withstand condemnation. I keep loving the person even though they may feel like an enemy. If I have been trained to offer healthy correction, I will be a gentle confronter. We are not loving our enemies when we leave them stuck in their destructive character.

Jesus commanded us to love our enemies and pray for those who persecute us (Matt. 5:44). Praying for someone who feels like an enemy helps us share their pain, which is the path out of Enemy Mode. When our pain sharing circuits get turned off, we must bring them back into full operation to exhibit Jesus' character.

By now, our group had been meeting for weeks. As we trained to notice Enemy Mode in our own lives, it became a regular topic of conversation for us. We would hear people share, "I sure went into Enemy Mode yesterday when my coworker blamed me for missing our deadline." We helped each other track our ventures into this dark mode and find the way out. We did this work in community.

Narcissists will resist receiving healthy correction. Since they are unable to feel special through relationships, they rely on accomplishments, position, and attractiveness. They use self-justification to defeat anyone who may seem to threaten their sense of being special. These strategies cause them to live most of their lives in Predatory Enemy Mode. They view the people around them in two ways: either people make them feel special or people are threats to them.

Immunizing Our Community

Now we see a fuller picture of why healthy soil is crucial, not only for character formation but also for resisting the growth of a relational disease. If our community is deeply bonded in joyful love, narcissistic trickery does not have the same power to separate us. Our joy tanks are full, so we have the capacity to handle great distress. Our love is steadfast because a *hesed* community has learned to suffer together. We share our weaknesses, so narcissistic criticisms do not intimidate us. We develop the capacity to love difficult people.

Our group identity is well developed, so when a leader uses

condemnation or self-justification to eliminate shame, we immediately spot this flaw. Our reaction is not to condemn the narcissist but to show love by offering correction. People with narcissistic tendencies will feel uncomfortable in our community because
they cannot manipulate our identities. Jesus alone is the standard
that we use to tell each other who we are and how we act. An
interloper gains no ground trying to corrupt our identity.

We gently and lovingly correct narcissists when they exhibit
behavior that looks nothing like how Jesus acted. We absolutely
refuse to give the narcissist a pass, because giving a pass would not
be loving. The narcissist might see our correction as toxic, but our
community has a culture of correction that promotes relational
health. This means that everyone is gently correcting everyone,
and no one stands out as particularly flawed. The narcissistic mind
sees many examples of people correcting each other and eagerly
receiving the reproof. Our joy, love, identity, and correction work
together to provide the narcissistic brain the examples it needs.

A church may be vulnerable to narcissists, but that does not
make it a narcissistic church. The weakness of this church is in
its soil. If you combine depleted soil with poor understanding of
maturity and the "drive to dominate," it becomes a matter of time
before a narcissist takes over. Paul describes a church that acqui-
esces to an abusive leader in 2 Corinthians 11:19–20: "You gladly
put up with fools since you are so wise! In fact, you even put up
with anyone who enslaves you or exploits you or takes advantage
of you or puts on airs or slaps you in the face." The Corinthians
lacked the nutrients in their soil to handle these defective leaders. They should have gently and firmly corrected them instead of
tolerating their behavior.

Seeing narcissism through the eyes of Scripture and brain
science helps us feel compassion for narcissists. They are caught
in a great weakness and do not realize it. Narcissists are not our

enemies. When we show them *hesed* in a Christlike group identity, diseased leaders learn how shame can improve their character. Instead of fearing and avoiding shame, they are shown how to metabolize it relationally: "We are glad to be with you in these feelings. We are glad we get to go through this together." Our joy, *hesed*, group identity, and correction combine to form a lifesaver that pulls the self-justifier to safety.[8] It may be necessary to remove a leader in order for them to heal. Their soul is more important than their job as a pastor. We must continue to welcome them in our loving community, without which they have little chance to heal.

This is some deep water, but there is good news in all of this talk about an infected Christianity. We have hope. The disease thrives in some communities and languishes in others. Half-brained churches are susceptible because they have weak soil. Full-brained churches have robust soil, and narcissism has trouble taking root.

This stiff-necked infection is a vicious relational weakness that is difficult but not impossible to treat. Treating a severe infection starts by restoring the health of the community soil. Jesus' vision for his church is a full-brained, vibrant, loving community.

Significant changes and work are required to create a community with sufficiently healthy soil to resist narcissism, but the disease can be stopped. The infection can be cured, narcissists can be healed, and narcissism can be eradicated from the church.

Lord Jesus, help us.

- -

**When we fail to fortify the relational soil of our churches,
we open ourselves to a destructive relational disease.
Our leaders focus on winning instead of building people**

up in their faith. Personalities grow large and cast a long shadow. Left unchecked, our churches drift so far from the character of Jesus that He no longer wants us to shine. He takes our lampstand away. Relationally rich soil gives a narcissist a chance to heal through loving community.

- -

GROUP DISCUSSION QUESTIONS

1. Complete the *Soil Sample 5: Narcissism Signs* in Appendix A for your Christian community. Discuss the signs of narcissism you see in your life and your community.
2. Read 3 John 9. Have you lived or worked with someone who needed to be first? Share your experiences of what it was like to interact with this person. How did he or she influence the dynamic of your group? Was their behavior ever corrected? If not, what kept you from speaking up?
3. Read the list of narcissistic behaviors enumerated in this chapter. Which ones have you seen played out in a Christian community? In your family? Which ones do you see in your own life?
4. In your opinion, how vulnerable is your church's soil to the relational infection of narcissism? Which of the soil ingredients is most lacking?

TRY IT OUT

1. Share a time in the last few weeks when you suspect you went into Enemy Mode. Look at the *Enemy Mode Checklist* in Appendix D and share whether you were in Simple Enemy Mode or Predatory Enemy Mode. What did it feel like when

you were in Enemy Mode? What did it feel like when you returned to Compassionate Relational Mode?

2. Make a group list of what gets you into Enemy Mode.

3. Make a group list of what gets us out of Enemy Mode and back to Relational Mode (see Appendix D for more information).

4. What are you learning (need to learn) while you are still in Enemy Mode so you can deliberately get yourself out?

FURTHER RESOURCES FOR THIS CHAPTER

Narcissism:

• E. James Wilder, *The Pandora Problem*

Exercises in spotting self-justification:

• Barbara Moon, *The Pandora Problem Companion Guide*

8

- - - - - - - - -

A Full-Brained Christianity

"'Love the Lord your God with all your heart and with all your soul and with all your strength and with all your mind'; and, 'Love your neighbor as yourself.'"

Luke 10:27

HAVING OUR EYES opened to the relational disease that grows in depleted soil, let's explore the alternative—the vibrant transformational community. Whole-brained Christianity makes full use of truth and relationship. Half-brained Christianity parks on the truth and leaves the relational soil untended.

Jesus wants a church with healthy soil that keeps relationships in the center. Each of the four ingredients of healthy soil is relational. Joy is what I feel when my brain senses that you are happy to be with me. *Hesed* is our family attachment of joyful love. Group identity is our corporate map of who we are and how we act as children of the living God. Our *culture of correction* leaves no man or woman behind. When someone forgets who they are, we bring them back gently to their true self. Healthy soil is relational through and through.

By building a foundation of relational joy, love, and identity, we create an environment where we naturally and regularly witness transformation. We expect radical change when people join our community. As we reintroduce right-brain practices into our discipleship—along with the traditional left-brain spiritual disciplines—we are using the full-brain power that God gave us to form our character. The Great Commission displaces the great omission as our people learn to obey Jesus with heart and mind. All of us eagerly accept correction when we stop acting like ourselves.

People choose to be involved in a particular Christian community for many reasons. The primary attraction of a full-brained community is our joy and love. People might not remark, "Their teaching is so good." "I love the music there." "That pastor is such a good teacher." Instead, they might say, "These people love each other so much." "This room is filled with joy." "I want to be like them." Love is the centerpiece of everything a full-brained church does. A church planted in rich relational soil may be less visually stimulating than other churches, but it is relationally stimulating. Being stimulated by love and joy is more important than being stimulated by other factors.

The Full-Brained Pastor

Unlike most Christian leaders, the relational pastor intentionally stays small. People are not impressed by this pastor, except by his humility and maturity. A full-brained community is impressed by Jesus alone and sees any attempt to magnify another person as an opportunity to offer a gentle rebuke. In a healthy church, people talk about Jesus all the time. They seldom talk about the pastor, and this is as it should be. Jesus is large and in charge. The pastor is but one of many people in a community where all faithfully complete the assignments Jesus gave them.

Pastors and other leaders stay small and act like trainers—laser focused on creating a relational environment that fosters transformation. Instead of looking only at attendance, giving, or other numbers, they also focus intently on bringing their people to maturity.

Much has been written of the exploits of the heroes of World War II, but what do you know about the drill sergeants who trained them in boot camp? Who was Beethoven's childhood piano teacher? Who first instructed Serena Williams how to hit a tennis ball? Who taught Lionel Messi to dribble a soccer ball? Trainers are seldom famous. A relational pastor remains largely unknown outside the church. His flock is thankful for the maturity they are developing. Pastors who refuse to be magnified know that their example will encourage the next generation of pastors to stay small—just like Jesus taught.

We can mistake the inflated pastor for a great leader if we believe the world's definition of greatness. Jesus operates under a different rubric. We find Him adjusting the disciples' definition when He catches them arguing about who is the greatest. The disciples are debating about which of them would be the biggest winner in the kingdom of heaven. They no doubt have images in their minds of what that looked like, but Jesus flips their picture upside down.

Jesus corrects the disciples by saying, "If anyone would be first, he must be last of all and servant of all" (Mark 9:35 ESV). Apparently, the disciples cannot accept this adjustment. It was too big of a stretch. Jesus must repeat His upside-down definition several times.

On another occasion Jesus calls a little child, placing the child in the middle of the disciples. The men probably looked at each other and wondered what Jesus was doing. With the child standing in the middle He explains, "Truly I tell you, unless you change and become like little children, you will never enter the kingdom of heaven. Therefore, whoever takes the lowly position of this child is the greatest in the kingdom of heaven" (Matt. 18:3–4). Jesus gives them a visual picture of a small child and basically says, "This is what greatness looks like." He also brings group identity into the picture. We stop acting like members of God's kingdom when we inflate ourselves and seek to be great.

His new definition still does not sink in, so Jesus repeats Himself yet again. He tells His disciples to observe how the Jewish religious leaders carefully manage their public images by parading in religious garments and welcoming titles of honor. Jesus then delivers a beautiful example of healthy correction:

> "But you are not to be called 'Rabbi,' for you have one Teacher, and you are all brothers. And do not call anyone on earth 'father,' for you have one Father, and he is in heaven. Nor are you to be called instructors, for you have one Instructor, the Messiah. The greatest among you will be your servant. For those who exalt themselves will be humbled, and those who humble themselves will be exalted." (Matt. 23:8–12)

We reject titles that seek to exalt in God's kingdom because they make no sense. We are a people who refuse to accept exaltation. I do not believe that Jesus forbids the titles "Rabbi, father, and instructor" in all situations. In the context, Jewish religious leaders were using these titles to gain praise and special treatment—to elevate themselves. We are careful not to use titles in a way that exalts a person. We are all just brothers and sisters, and we magnify the one head of our church—Jesus the Messiah. He is our only hero, and we have no other. His Father is our only Father. They stay big, and we stay small. Why is this so hard for us to understand?

Does our use of religious titles agree or disagree with Jesus' definition of greatness? Paul uses appropriate titles for rulers outside the church as a matter of respect.[1] Inside the church, however, Paul uses family language. "But we were gentle among you, like a nursing mother taking care of her own children" (1 Thess. 2:7 ESV). Paul calls himself the "father" of the Corinthians. The context indicates that he was using this term as a form of endearment, not elevation. It is true that Paul calls himself an apostle, but this is not a title that would exalt him above others. An apostle is a messenger. Paul is a messenger sent by Jesus. None of the apostles use this title to express exalted status.

Not only do Christian leaders reject titles of exaltation, the whole community must learn not to elevate our leaders. I do not believe that Jesus is issuing a blanket rejection of these titles, but we need to at least ask ourselves whether we might be using them in the way Jesus is warning us against. Christians need to be instructed here with Jesus' words and wisdom.

The word *pastor* is used on many pages of this book. Are we using this title correctly? We need to ask ourselves, "Are we using this title to elevate a person?" If so, we may need to consider Jesus' teaching in Matthew 23. However, if we are using *pastor* to name the task Jesus has assigned certain people, then we are using it correctly. After all, a pastor is a shepherd who tenderly cares for and protects the sheep.

Unfortunately, we often build and arrange our churches in ways that can magnify the leader. During many services, the church leader is elevated, standing above the crowd. Do families act like this? We hang large screens above the stage to magnify their face as the Teacher. Their enormous image looms above us as we listen to them dispense wisdom. Do families act like this? The use of video magnification in a church may be necessary, but pastors should simultaneously be modeling "image shrinkifica-tion" more often. Leaders are not exempt from Jesus' upside-down definition of greatness. We, pastors, should be willing to rethink what we do and why we do it.

Emotionally mature leaders always keep relationships more important than ministry. They never sacrifice their congregation's *hesed* attachments in order to "do great things." The horse remains firmly in front of the cart, and every task or ministry they perform flows from abundant *hesed*.

In fact, an important skill for pastors to learn is how to live in joyful *hesed* with God and each other. I was never taught this in seminary. The focus on love assures that life (from this point on) will be rooted in love. This *hesed*-centered paradigm requires significant rewiring of the way we think and live.

Pastors who openly share their weaknesses and admit when they feel underqualified and overwhelmed are building *hesed* and modeling how to stay small. They also readily ask for help from others to change their own character. Healthy leaders look for opportunities to show their smallness and weakness. This is, of course, much easier said than done. It makes sense to start practic-ing vulnerability in a smaller group. A small group curriculum can have steps to teaching people to share weakness. Leaders model how to humbly become little children. Too many leaders demon-strate the exact opposite—they show us how to be winners. The disciples wanted to be winners, debating who was the greatest, but Jesus would have none of it. His kingdom does not work that way.

Pastors of whole-brained churches are first and foremost trainers. Ephesians 4:11–13 teaches that the primary job of Chris-tian leaders is building people up to maturity, the very task so often neglected. Leaders must do their own relational training. They are not perfect, but they are becoming mature. Healthy pastors model maturity, so they must possess it first. Half-brained discipleship passes on information and techniques. Whole-brained disciple-ship uses all the resources of every generation in the community to develop mature character. There is no title or position of honor that lets you skip this training.

A whole-brained church releases transformed disciples into the world like cottonwood seeds in the Colorado wind. Invigorated disciples plant new life in the culture wherever they land. Jesus dispersed His disciples around the world after training them for three years. These disciples and their spiritual descendants changed the fabric of the world. Likewise, we pastors do not focus on changing the world ourselves. Instead, we are trainers who focus on building Christlike character into our people. If we do our job well, our people will change the world.

Training

A full-brained training starts by building healthy soil, but it does not end there. Rich relational soil creates the perfect environment for character to sprout and thrive, but there is much work still to do. Full-brained churches realize this and take training seriously. Spiritual and emotional training must be done in healthy soil for it to be effective. We start by enriching the soil so that everything we plant can thrive, but our discipleship does not end there.

My first exposure to this new training started when I asked a simple question: "Give me an example of a practice that strength-ens my brain in a way that makes me more like Jesus." Jim had us stand up and learn a reggae rhythm that had four beats:

> Rest
> Clap
> Clap-clap
> Clap

Then we gathered into groups of three and went around the circle clapping the four-beat rhythm. It confused me at first. We were a group of three clapping a four-part rhythm as we went around the circle. Each time around the circle, I would have a different clapping part:

Me: Rest
Bob: Clap
John: Clap-clap
Me: Clap
Bob: Rest
John: Clap
Me: Clap-clap
Bob: Clap

I needed to concentrate because my part would change each time we went around the circle. I remember thinking, *This is weird. Why is he having us clap? What does this have to do with discipleship?* Then, as though he were reading my mind, Jim told us to replace the "rest" with an attempt to experience God's presence during that beat.

Me: Connect with God
Bob: Clap
John: Clap-clap
Me: Clap
Bob: Connect with God
John: Clap
Me: Clap-clap
Bob: Clap

Jim explained, "This exercise is designed to train us to experience God's presence in a distracting environment. Jesus did this very well, and we must train ourselves to be like Jesus." I thought of myself and how easily I lose track of God's presence when I am in a distracting situation. It never occurred to me that I could train to do that.

My wife and I are two years into a full-brain discipleship training designed by Jim Wilder and others. I will take you through a quick explanation of what this training entails. You may not understand everything I share, but I want to give you a 10,000-foot view of a full-brain discipleship program. This section will give you a taste of new practices so that you can have an idea of what is available. Further training will be necessary to gain the skill I am sharing (see Further Resources for this Chapter and the endnotes for further learning[2]).

The first step in our training program was increasing our joy capacity. You learned why joy is crucial in chapter 3. Building joy starts with disciplines of gratitude. I also practiced building non-verbal facial joy with my wife. We learned to feel the cues in our bodies when joy was rising.

At times, our joy seemed overwhelming, so we also learned how to quiet our nervous systems. We learned various exercises involving breathing, tapping our bodies, and yawning. They were weird for me at first, but I could feel their calming effect. The inability to quiet oneself is a leading predictor of mental illness. Quieting ourselves allows us to digest the joy we build, much like resting after a hard workout allows our muscles to rest and build new capacity. We also learned how to calm ourselves in the big emotions. Learning to quiet myself was a new skill for me, and I found it difficult. Yes, you can train yourself to do this.

I assessed my maturity level in detail and started filling in any holes. Our brain progresses through maturity levels as we complete the necessary skills for each stage. The maturity levels are Infant, Child, Adult, Parent, and Elder.[3] There are ten to twenty relational skills to be learned at each stage. For example, one infant skill is "Important needs were met until I learned to ask." If my important needs were not met, my brain did not develop an important skill that I will need for the rest of my life. I have a hole in my relational skills.

Most of us have parents who did not learn all of these skills themselves, and our parents' holes leave holes in our maturity. We must go back and fill missing emotional and relational skills in order to completely move on to the next stage. I found holes in my Infant and Child maturity levels that I am in the process of repairing. This felt humiliating to me at first, but I got over it (see Appendix E for more).

I am training to stay joyful in the six big emotions that our brain recognizes—sadness, fear, anger, shame, disgust, and despair. I'm not training to be joyful instead of sad or angry. I'm training to be joyful in the midst of unpleasant emotions by developing the neural pathway between these big emotions and joy. We learned in chapter 3 that being joyful means staying relationally connected to people who are glad to be with us, even when we are in distress. Yes, you need to train yourself to do that.

I am learning to act like myself in the big six emotions. If we have holes in our maturity, our personality can change when we are in distress. "You won't like me when I'm angry" really means that I become a different person when experiencing anger. This is a right-hemisphere malfunction that can be corrected. I am training to never become a person other than who I am, even in deep distress. Yes, you can train yourself to do that. You can train yourself to be angry and loving at the same time. This has been hard for me to learn, but I am making progress.

We learn to tell each other stories in a way that activates our nervous systems with any of the big six emotions. These stories have the effect of treading a path between a big emotion and joy.

Connecting all our emotions to joy is done primarily by storytelling, not by teaching. We need examples to imitate, not facts to memorize. Our character is formed by stories, so a Great Commission church is a storytelling church. However, not all stories touch our character. There are particular characteristics of a story that activate our nervous systems, so we need to practice this skill. Let me give you an example.

One of the big emotions is anger. While writing this book, I unintentionally put my editing program in a state where all of the letters turned red and underlined. All sorts of formatting codes appeared and cluttered up the entire document. I searched the internet to find how to get my document back to normal. The instructions I followed ended up deleting all of our editor's comments, which are crucial for me. I found out that once deleted, comments are irretrievable. I lost an entire day of work under a tight deadline. I had to go back to my latest backup. I felt my head heat up and build pressure. My heart started beating so hard I could feel it in my skin. I realized that I was angry and that it was building. I needed another person's help, so I shared my anger with my wife. She was very kind and said, "That it so frustrating! I am so sorry." I could feel the effect of my wife's compassion as my heart slowed down and my head cooled. I was still angry, but I was not alone in my anger. My wife helped me control my frustration.

You may not realize it, but this story was told in a way to help your nervous system learn to connect to someone in anger. The story would be even more effective in person so that you could see the emotion on my face as I tell it.

I am cleaning up childhood trauma using a full-brain procedure that brings the perspective of Jesus into my trauma.[4] This exercise trains the control center in my right hemisphere to sense the presence and perspective of Jesus, even in my darkest memories. The presence of Jesus helps metabolize the emotional energy of trauma. Sharing what I learn from Jesus about my trauma with other people (more storytelling) helps my brain create a new library entry that eliminates future triggering. As a result of this practice, distressing situations no longer trigger a huge emotional response in me. I often think, *That would have been an emotional avalanche a few years ago.* My resilience has improved significantly by learning to see my wounds from Jesus' perspective.

Dallas Willard and others write about learning to live the "with God" life, where we practice God's presence moment-by-moment.[5] I liked the sound of that, but I could never pull it off in my distracting life. The same trauma exercise described in the previous paragraph has taught me how to experience God's presence more consistently than I have before.

I am learning to diagnose when the control center in my brain has gone into the ditch and how to get myself unstuck. Not only am I learning to diagnose myself; I am also being trained to diagnose others. Here are some of the signs that others are stuck:

- They can't see that they are part of the problem
- They are making decisions based on their fears
- They are stuck in one of the big six emotions
- They are confused about how to act like themselves

These are a few of the more obvious signs almost everyone has experienced and seen in others.

I am learning to help other people when their relational control center gets stuck, which happens to all of us. For pastors, being able to diagnose is an especially important skill, because people will occasionally desynchronize during discipleship exercises. Helping them recover and understand what just happened might be the difference between an effective and ineffective training. This skill requires more wisdom, training, and maturity than can be listed here.

We also exercise the left hemisphere, learning to spot malfunctions in our thinking and correct them quickly. A left-brain malfunction occurs when my thoughts do not line up with reality. Sometimes, when emotions are big or trauma gets triggered, our beliefs detach from reality: "God has abandoned me. I'm all alone!" There are many reasons why our thoughts get corrupted, and a full-brain training helps us troubleshoot these malfunctions and remove mental roadblocks. Removing false beliefs has greatly enhanced my enjoyment of reading and studying Scripture.

Finally, I am learning to recognize Enemy Mode and practice getting out of it. This is an essential exercise to help us love our enemies. The first step is to recognize when I am in one of the Enemy Modes and then learn how to get back into Relational Mode as quickly as possible. We use the term *Relational Mode* to describe the healthy operating mode of our brain. When we train ourselves to recognize and get out of Enemy Mode, we grow the ability to love difficult people.

For example, our homework one week was to record how many times we found ourselves going into Enemy Mode. This honed our ability to recognize what it feels like to shift out of Relational Mode. It was eye-opening for me to see how many times I caught myself going into Enemy Mode in a week. It was humbling, too.

In one instance, I was in the left turn lane waiting to merge onto a highway. The lane was backed up because the driver at the front could not seem to find a hole in oncoming traffic and make the turn. I felt my face heating up and my impatience growing. I was late for a meeting. Finally, I yelled out loud in my car, "Go! You can easily turn left now! Come on!" Then I realized I was in Enemy Mode. I no longer cared about relationships. I just wanted to solve the problem, even if I trampled on someone with my words. I had been doing this much of my life without knowing. Now it no longer feels normal, and I catch myself more quickly.

Once I realize that I am in Enemy Mode, there is a suite of exercises to help me become relational again. The first step is to share the pain of the other person. In my car, I imagined a time when I froze and could not make a decision. What I would have wanted in that situation is someone to show compassion and patience. Slowly, I could feel the Enemy Mode losing its grip on my mind as I felt compassion for the driver. My relational circuits were coming back online, and I was returning to relational thinking.

We also learned to detect when another person is in Enemy Mode and gently help them get back to their relational self. My wife and I have given each other permission to point out when we suspect the other has slipped into Enemy Mode. Here are some familiar signs of a person in Enemy Mode:

- Self-justification
- Condemnation received or given
- Lack of judgment
- No pain sharing
- Forgotten *hesed* (if there was any)
- Loss of group identity awareness
- Disconnection from God even when hearing Scripture[6]

We must have well developed maturity to be able to help a person in Enemy Mode, or we will get stuck ourselves. Like helping a drowning swimmer, if we are not well trained, we will get pulled under trying to help. It is easy to see how this skill makes a church resistant to narcissistic behavior. When people have been trained, we recognize Enemy Mode quickly and do not let it run rampant.

Results

Whew! You may not be able to take all that in, but let me explain the results I see in my own life.

First, I feel different. I fell more connected to my body. I can feel God in my body and experience His love viscerally. I feel the warmth of His love even as I type this sentence. My mind is less cluttered and I am triggered less often. Experiences that would previously have obstructed me no longer have the emotional energy they once stored. I am better able to regulate my emotions so that they don't go haywire as often. I'm not perfect, but I know how to handle my malfunctions. My failures no longer puzzle me like they did before. Instead of wondering, *Why did I do that?* or *Why did I just say that?* I know how to debug my own failures.

When I do get stuck, which still happens, I eagerly bring my weakness to my community, and we work on it together. I now look at my malfunctions as opportunities to let God train me and heal me. When I see a failure in my own life, my first thought now is, *I wonder what God wants me to learn from this?* I thank God for my malfunctions, because working on them often results in a growth spurt. I have grown more in the last two years than in the previous twenty, and I attribute this directly to my training.

Some of you may think, *This is too complicated. I just want to go to church, sing some songs, and hear a good message from the Bible. Then I want to go home and watch the Broncos game."* If so, this training is not for you, but character transformation will not be for you, either. The only way this training does not work is if you do not do it.

Full-Brained Worship

Since relationships infuse everything we do in a full-brained community, we view music differently. We believe this is a return to the full-brained use of music found in the New Testament that has been lost over the last three hundred years. Paul writes in Colossians 3:16, "Let the message of Christ dwell among you richly as you teach and admonish one another with all wisdom through . . ." If you had never read this chapter of Colossians before, how would you finish Paul's sentence? What do we use to teach and admonish each other with wisdom? Sermons? Bible Study? Reading Scripture? Conferences? Paul finishes the sentence by saying that we teach each other wisdom through "psalms, hymns, and songs from the Spirit, singing to God with gratitude in your hearts." In another letter, Paul adds, "speaking to one another with psalms, hymns, and songs from the Spirit. Sing and make music from your heart to the Lord" (Eph. 5:19).

I have attended numerous churches where the modern concept of worship involves singing songs to God, but it often leaves out singing to each other. I was fascinated when Jim explained the neuroscience of singing songs to each other. Remember from chapter 1 that sensory input enters our brain at the back of the right hemisphere. When we sing to each other, the words, the melody, the sound from musical instruments, and the expressions on our faces as we all sing enter our back-right hemisphere and travel forward. The right side is nonverbal, so the words flow to the front without being fully processed, but the other input is full of material that creates right-brain imagery. Facial expressions, melody, and the relational tone of our community as we all sing stimulate our right brains to build joy, relational attunement, character, and identity.

All the stimulus from the song takes a hard left turn behind our right eye, and the words are interpreted as they travel front to back on the left side. When we sing to one another, we are engaging in full-brained worship!

None of the churches I have attended were configured to sing to one another. Seating is designed to fit the maximum number of people efficiently in a given space in order to receive teaching. Seats are aligned in rows facing toward the stage. We are led in worship by people we might not even know. Our brains respond differently to this impersonal worship than if we were singing to each other in a *hesed* community. I do not mean to imply that full-brained worship is impossible in our current church configuration, but we must be open to making changes in our churches and meetings that enhance our relational development, including how we worship. We must use the imagination and creativity that God gives us to solve these problems.

The full-brained church maintains a high-joy environment with lots of play, freedom, creativity, and the safety to fail. Mature leadership creates and maintains this environment.

Getting Off the Hamster Wheel

In many churches I have attended, the pastors are so loaded down with responsibilities and activities that they can barely keep up. Like a hamster running in an exercise wheel, many pastors run frantically just to keep the machinery of the church going. They quickly become exhausted and burn out. This imbalance of responsibility is not a biblical model.

Because of the common upside-down view of greatness in our culture, a full-brained church must become more decentralized, and responsibilities distributed. The pastor is not exalted as the ultimate leader and expert on all matters. The community functions like an interdependent network of equals—like a family. Elders, the most mature members of the church, are responsible for handling conflicts and debugging the stickiest problems.

Although I am a parent of three children and do more work maintaining the household than my children do, I make sure they share enough of the chores to help them grow and carry some of the responsibilities. As they grow, I give them more to do. Churches that function as spiritual families will have elders who spread responsibilities around, ensuring that everyone is involved and growing. Elders pay attention when a person is ready to be challenged. Elders are always looking to nurture their people. Church structure begins to resemble a spiritual family with *hesed* attachments.[7]

Paul shares a healthy model when he describes a typical church meeting in 1 Corinthians 14:26. This is the only place in Scripture describing a typical church gathering. "When you come together, each of you has a hymn, or a word of instruction, a revelation, a tongue or an interpretation. Everything must be done so that the church may be built up." The phrase "each of you" should be ringing in your ears. When Paul refers to "each of you," he is not just referring to leaders or staff. He addresses this letter "to the church of God in Corinth, to those sanctified in Christ Jesus and called to be his holy people, together with all those everywhere who call on the name of our Lord Jesus Christ" (1 Cor. 1:2). He is writing to everyone.

Paul instructs each member of the church to contribute something—a song, a word of teaching, a revelation, a tongue, or an interpretation. Teaching is not reserved for the select few, and everyone else is shuffled off to do children's ministry or parking duty. Ministry is spread around, and everyone is involved. Mature elders and leaders ensure that the meeting stays focused on building up everyone.

Paul's model may appear chaotic to modern readers, and, indeed, Paul spent significant energy handling the chaos in the churches he planted. He must have understood the importance of getting everyone involved, even if this presents problems from time to time. If church leaders desire to follow Paul's example, they would effectively eliminate the line between clergy and laypeople.

Maturity

Notice that Paul keeps his eye on the ball in his description of a typical church meeting. "Everything must be done so that the church may be built up" (1 Cor. 14:26). He never forgets the ultimate purpose—maturity. The Great Commission requires a steadfast focus on building character. The healthy relational soil that we have been studying creates the ideal environment for building maturity.

The negative headlines we read about the public failures of Christians are usually the result of immaturity. When a pastor's character flaws get him fired, we often hear people say, "He needs to take some time off to get healing." While healing may be part of the path to wholeness, what this leader really needs is maturity. Their community must help him walk through his missing maturity skills and show him a new way to live. All the healing in the world will not make a person mature.

My wife, Claudia, moved from Argentina after we married, slowly adjusting to her new country. She called me from the supermarket one day, sounding exasperated. "I want to make empanadas for dinner and I need flour. In my country, I buy flour. Here I am in the flour aisle and I see white four, wheat flour, self-rising flour, and more. There are twenty types of flour! Which should I buy for empanadas?"

How many types of maturity are there? It is more complex than we may think. Is maturity the same when we are two, twenty-two, and eighty-two years old? Do you want spiritual maturity, emotional maturity, relational maturity, junior-high maturity, average male maturity, or what? We think there must be a few different traits involved. It never occurs to us that there are layers of detail in maturity.

Christians may define maturity as a lack of visible sin or equate it to a knowledge of Scripture. Many of us unwisely assign maturity to a person who has occupied a church position for a long time. We often look at someone who is gifted and anointed, and assume that maturity must be behind their successful ministry. But maturity and giftedness may not go together.

The full-brained church has a robust definition of maturity and how to bring a person up through the levels so they are constantly maturing. Leaving maturity to chance is a fatal error in leadership. Every member and especially every leader does the hard work of filling in their maturity gaps. We do this work in community because it requires copious amounts of *hesed*.

Part of our full-brain training program involves studying the lists of skills for each maturity level and assessing our own maturity. Last week, our group walked through the Infant Maturity skills together—for the third time in a year. We stopped on each skill, one by one, and shared how we were doing. When we found holes in our relational skills, we shared our strategies to fill them and tracked our progress. Many of our plans of action involved the help of other members of our group. I made the following request of my team: "I need you all to share stories of when you stayed relational in shame and despair. I need your help with this because my parents did not model this to me." Each person in our group is aware of the strengths and weaknesses in the maturity of each other. There is great freedom in this openness (see Appendix E for more on maturity levels).

Some churches marginalize certain people because it threatens their sense of purity when a prostitute or a transgender person walks through the doors. A full-brained church with a robust discipleship program welcomes anyone who wants to come in, knowing that there's a path to maturity for everyone. Maturity and healing are not left to chance. Everyone in the community has the opportunity to be transformed into the image of Christ.

Some churches openly welcome all people, even people with messy lives, but they offer no real path to maturity. There is no plan in the church to form anyone, much less a deeply broken person, into the image of Christ. People can show up to some meetings and hear some inspiring talks, but they are on their own in building their emotional and relational skills. There is no plan to help them mature. This is the void of the great omission, where we make Christians but not disciples.

The world sees the word *immature* as an insult, but when we understand the roots of immaturity, we treat it with compassion. A full-brained community has a different attitude toward immaturity. Since we cannot transfer maturity by teaching, we must possess it ourselves to give it to our children. When our parents have holes in their maturity, these holes get passed to us as infants and children.

Many of our missing maturity skills needed to be developed before the age of four when so many of a child's abilities are developing. Imagine a four-year-old who cannot speak, talk, or use the bathroom. We would know something is wrong. But it is equally true when they cannot quiet themselves, follow instruction, or manage their temper tantrums. We, as infants, needed to be taught many emotional skills so we are not responsible for all of our developmental holes. A two-year-old is not responsible for missing maturity skills. Let me say this again, because we have difficulty believing it. *We are not responsible for the holes in our immaturity.* We *are* responsible, however, for repairing the holes later in life. It is not our sin when our caregivers did not give us emotional skills we needed during the first four years of life. While immaturity will make it easier for us to sin, immaturity is not sin. Few churches see building maturity as part of their task. The consequences of a church failing to do this work are devastating.[8]

When I am mature, I eagerly accept correction and can receive other people's input on my life because I am not defensive (learned during Child Stage). My personality does not change even when my emotions are distressing (learned during Infant Stage). I can satisfy my own and others' needs (learned during Adult Stage). I can give life to others without resenting it (learned during Parent Stage). I can take care of my community without neglecting my own family (learned during Elder Stage). I am emotionally and relationally resilient (learned during Infant Stage). I know how to resolve conflict while staying relationally connected (expands during every stage). I have no addictions—a sign of infant level maturity.[9] Our maturity has absolutely nothing to do with our value or God's love for us.

Narcissism and the Full-Brained Community

We must have solid maturity to deal with narcissism because it is a character flaw that can be corrected only by better character. Narcissism is evidence of holes in infant level maturity—an inability to handle shame. We cannot teach someone the way out of narcissism. We must model better character.

Like any group of people, a full-brained community will find their members exhibiting narcissistic behavior, but this group is well prepared to handle it. Narcissism is a "shame dysfunction," and a *hesed* community is a place where shame will be treated kindly. This community provides a chance for the narcissist to build a pathway between shame and joy, which is required to heal narcissism. Our community will gently correct narcissistic behaviors when they arise, since everyone is open to having their character adjusted, including pastors and leaders. There are no untouchables in a community with healthy relational soil. We all freely correct each other.

When people in a high-*hesed* community see a leader who accomplishes impressive things but who does not exhibit the character of Jesus, they do not justify the person. Members refuse to form a bubble of enablement around this leader. As the apostle John taught, "Whoever claims to live in him must live as Jesus did" (1 John 2:6). There is no excuse for good ministry to be accomplished with bad character, especially a lack of love. This community will not allow that. Love is valued above all other character traits.

When people justify themselves in response to being corrected, we will gently remind them that self-justification has no place in God's kingdom. We all accept correction in our community because this is the path to transformation. Our refusal to let anyone justify themselves neutralizes the narcissist's favorite tool. If they can learn to abandon their self-justifications, they are on the path to recovery.

In this community, we realize that a *hesed* attachment with the narcissist is key. We must love them well, or our attempts to help them will be rebuffed. Narcissists are well armed to keep shame away. Neurologically, our attachment center is the deepest part of our brain, and this design allows our love to get under the narcissist's armor. Our *hesed* for the narcissist is neurologically deeper than their defenses, so their attachment center gets activated before their defenses wake up.

We must do the hard work on our own hearts to be able to love them, because narcissists are challenging to love. Building and maintaining *hesed* in the presence of narcissism is a difficult and tricky task requiring well-developed character. We also need a community with healthy soil because narcissism does not respond well to one-on-one treatment. The bubble community surrounding a narcissist needs to be popped and replaced by a *hesed* community of mature people. This requires the community to build a strong group identity using exercises provided in *The Pandora Problem Companion Guide* (see Resources at the end of the chapter). The group's well-formed group identity must be strong enough to untangle the narcissistic knots in the person's character.

- -

FACING NARCISSISM SAFELY

- We must remember God is with us and purifies our lives
- We must share rule over our dominion (from as small as our body to as large as our kingdom) with God
- We must speak up to the people in our identity group by correcting their worthless lies about glory that instead create shame
- We must actively stop the lies we love
- We must ensure anger does not lead to sin making us less than our joyful, *hesed* identity would inspire
- We must consult our hearts
- We need clean *hesed*
- We must quiet ourselves

Taken from *The Pandora Problem*, page 145

- -

The counseling community tends to view narcissism as an incurable condition. According to this view, we need to treat narcissism like cancer—cut it out and toss it away. We respectfully disagree. Narcissism is a character deficiency, and the narcissist needs a loving community that is happy to be with them, even when they stop acting like a Christian. We love them but do not give them a free pass in their character dysfunction. We have this same attitude toward everyone in our community, so the narcissist gets many chances to see others being corrected. A culture of correction lowers the intensity of shame because everyone has their character corrected. No one is singled out as a defective person to be rebuked. We all have defects, and we also love each other deeply. We may need to remove a narcissist from their leadership position, but we still love them deeply.

Admittedly, many leaders will head for the hills once they realize that their narcissistic strategies will no longer protect them. A full-brained community can offer healing, but fear will overwhelm many narcissists. The level of *hesed* these leaders have with their community will likely determine whether they stay or go. Once they conclude that their schemes will not work in this soil, *hesed* is the only glue with the strength to keep them from leaving. *Hesed* is their lifeline.

The Great Opportunity

The very qualities that make a community resistant to narcissism also make it a healthy and vibrant witness in our world. Too many churches unintentionally end up following and copying the culture instead of modeling a better way to live. A community that is overflowing with joy and love stands out in the world.

When we combine our *hesed* with a strong identity, we hone who we are and how we act in everyday life. We develop a clear picture of what kind of people we are. We develop our identity together, both by reminding and correcting each other. A community with a strong group identity stands out in a fragmented culture that has no cohesive narrative of why we exist and how we act. Since our group identity is molded by the character of Jesus, we are displaying His light with our identity. A group identity that can withstand the manipulations of a narcissist is rooted in Jesus and His character. We present an attractive picture of heaven on earth.

When we refuse to justify ourselves or accept the justifications of others, we remove a common barrier to our growth. Instead, we openly share our weaknesses and invite feedback when we fail. Our community nurtures a "culture of correction" where, like Jesus, our radar is on. We are constantly scanning our community for opportunities to mold character.

The crowning glory of this community is that we are learning to love our enemies. The yardstick for measuring how we are progressing in our discipleship is looking at how well we love the difficult people in our lives. Loving our enemies is also the perfect practice for making our communities resistant to narcissism.

In popular media, Christians are often depicted as being judgmental of others and ignorant of their own poor behavior. A narcissism-resistant church turns that on its head. We stay in Relational Mode and invite people, even those who may feel like enemies, into our loving spiritual family.

A church that is trained to love their enemies is prepared to love anyone. People change through relational attachment much more than by winning an argument. When our relational soil contains the ingredients for growing enemy-lovers, it also becomes a church that shines the vibrant character of Jesus into a dark world. Jesus knows how to love His enemies, and He calls us to do the same, even when our enemies are narcissists.

We are living in a time of great opportunity. Not only are we recovering the lost task of discipleship, we also have insights into how God created our brains that no previous generation has had. We understand for the first time how our Creator designed our brains to form our character into the image of His Son. The relational soil described in this book is not the idea of any brilliant human being. The ingredients of healthy soil are based on the neurological circuits that God intricately fashioned and embedded with His image. We find the nutrients of healthy soil taught in Scripture and lived out in the life of Jesus. He has given us the great corrective to what was eroded over the last four hundred years since the Enlightenment. Yes, we are living in a time of great opportunity. The mysteries of love, applied to the way the brain learns, offer us hope for overcoming our spiritual stagnation and becoming whole-brained Christians.

GROUP DISCUSSION QUESTIONS

1. What changes might you make to your gatherings so that they appear more like Paul's description in 1 Corinthians 14:26?
2. Think of the four ingredients of healthy relational soil and evaluate your current Christian community. Where is your community strong, and where does your soil need improvement?
3. Read Colossians 3:16 and Ephesians 5:19. Does your church intentionally teach and build wisdom by singing? Do you ever sing to each other as part of your discipleship?

TRY IT OUT

Find the classic hymn "The Servant Song," and practice singing it to each other. Over the following week, try writing a new verse to include a specific aspect of your group identity. Try it out on each other and have fun with it. Here is an example we wrote about loving our enemies:

> I will help you love your enemies;
> see in them what God can see.

I'll help you find Christ's love within you;
help me find Christ's love in me.

Break up into groups of three and practice the reggae exercise mentioned in this chapter.

FURTHER RESOURCES FOR THIS CHAPTER

Maturity:
- Friesen, Wilder, Bierling, Koepcke, and Poole, *Living from the Heart Jesus Gave You*
- E. James Wilder, *The Complete Guide to Living with Men* (currently out of print, but copies may still be found)
- Visit www.thrivetoday.org for more information on maturity training

Cleaning up emotional messages from the past and healing trauma:
- Wilder, Kang, Loppnow, and Loppnow, *Joyful Journey: Listening to Immanuel*
- *Passing the Peace After a Crisis*, Life Model Works
- The extensive writings and videos of Karl D. Lehman, MD, at KCLehman.com. This material is more technical than that in *Joyful Journey*.

Relational skills training:
- My wife and I are going through Thrive, a full-brained relational skills training (thrivetoday.org/thrive).
- For exercises to help us with narcissism, our own and others', see Barbara Moon, *The Pandora Problem Companion Guide*

Appendix A

- - - - - - - - - -

Soil Assessment Questions

Q1: How much intention to improve is there?
Q2: How aware are you of experiencing this?
Q3: Observable sign
Q4: Observable sign
Q5: Observable sign
    Item score: None=0, Low=1, Medium=2, High=3
    Five items per scale = total score 15 (range 0–15)

SCALES

S1: Relational Joy
S2: *Hesed*
S3: Group Identity
S4: Correction
S5: Narcissism
    Scale score (add the 5 questions): 0–5 Low (1), 6–10 Medium (2), 11–15 High (3)
    Total test score (4 combined scales) range 4–12 (minus narcissism score = 1–11 range)

Soil Sample 1: Relational Joy Level

Pick a group or church where you participate regularly to complete this questionnaire.

Q1: In the last year, how much have you been encouraged or taught to intentionally raise relational joy there?
None=0, Low=1, Medium=2, High=3   Answer _____

Q2: In the last year, how aware have you been of "glad to be together" moments with other group members?
None=0, Low=1, Medium=2, High=3   Answer _____

Q3: Do you often feel faces light up when you come together in your community?
No=0, Rarely=1, Occasionally=2, Usually=3   Answer _____

Q4: How often do you share meals with people in your group?
Never=0, Rarely=1, Occasionally=2, Often=3   Answer _____

Q5: Does your group train you to increase joy through practices of gratitude?
None=0, Low=1, Medium=2, High=3   Answer _____

Add your answers for a total _____

Scoring your soil sample scale

Add the scores for the five questions. (Your total should be between 0 and 15)

If your total was 0 to 5 your scale score = 1 (Low joy)

If your total was 6 to 10 your scale score = 2 (Medium joy)

If your total was 11 to 15 your scale score = 3 (High joy)

Soil Sample 2: *Hesed* Attachment Development

Answer these questions about the group or church where you participate regularly.

Q1: In the last year, how much have you been encouraged or taught to intentionally form strong and eternal attachments?
None=0, Low=1, Medium=2, High=3   Answer ____

Q2: In the last year, have members moved toward better, lifelong relationships with the people in their lives?
No=0, A little=1, Somewhat=2, Substantially=3   Answer ____

Q3: How much effort is made in your community if something goes wrong or people stop attending?
None=0, Low=1, Medium=2, High=3   Answer ____

Q4: How often do you feel comfortable sharing a weakness or failure in this community?
Never=0, A little=1, Sometimes=2, Often=3   Answer ____

Q5: How often do you get to spend unhurried, unstructured time with people in your church or group whom you consider to be more mature Christians?
Never=0, Rarely=1, monthly=2, weekly or more=3   Answer ____

               Add your answers for a total _____

Scoring your soil sample scale

Add the scores for the five questions. (Your total should be between 0 and 15)

If your total was 0 to 5 your scale score = 1 (Low *hesed*)

If your total was 6 to 10 your scale score = 2 (Medium *hesed*)

If your total was 11 to 15 your scale score = 3 (High *hesed*)

Soil Sample 3: Group Identity Strength

Answer these questions about the group or church where you participate regularly.

Q1: In the last year, how much have you been encouraged or taught to intentionally speak with one another about who you really are as a group?

None=0, Low=1, Medium=2, High=3   Answer _____

Q2: In the last year, how satisfied are you with the way your group handles both good and bad times in your lives?

Not at all=0, Low=1, Medium=2, High=3   Answer _____

Q3: Anyone in your group could state the important aspects of who you are (not simply what you believe) and how others can tell by watching you.

No one=0, Rare=1, Some=2, Most=3   Answer _____

Q4: How often do you wonder, *What should I do in this situation?* and find a good answer from your community?

Never=0, Rarely=1, Occasionally=2, Often=3   Answer _____

Q5: How often have you seen another mature Christian act in a way that makes you think, *So that is how a follower of Jesus acts in that situation. I want to be like them?*

Never=0, Rarely=1, Occasionally=2, Often=3   Answer _____

Add your answers for a total _____

Scoring your soil sample scale

Add the scores for the five questions. (Your total should be between 0 and 15)

> If your total was 0 to 5 your scale score = 1 (Low group identity)
>
> If your total was 6 to 10 your scale score = 2 (Medium group identity)
>
> If your total was 11 to 15 your scale score = 3 (High group identity)

Soil Sample 4: "Culture of Correction" Assessment

Answer these questions about the group or church where you participate regularly.

Q1: In the last year, how much have you been encouraged or taught to intentionally remind members of your group "who we are" when one of you forgets?

  None=0, Low=1, Medium=2, High=3   Answer _____

Q2: In the last year, have you appreciated or seen others appreciate being corrected?

  No=0, Rarely=1, Occasionally=2, Frequently=3   Answer _____

Q3: Leadership encourages and receives correction from everyone.

  None=0, Low=1, Medium=2, High=3   Answer _____

Q4: How often do you hear teaching about the importance of acting like yourself?

  Never=0, A little=1, Occasionally=2, Often=3   Answer _____

Q5: How often do you notice a flaw in your own character and ask someone to help you to correct this flaw?

Never=0, A little=1, Occasionally=2, Often=3   Answer _____

Add your answers for a total _____

Scoring your soil sample scale

Add the scores for the five questions. (Your total should be between 0 and 15)

If your total was 0 to 5 your scale score = 1 (Low correction)

If your total was 6 to 10 your scale score = 2 (Medium correction)

If your total was 11 to 15 your scale score = 3 (High correction)

Soil Sample 5: Narcissism Signs

Answer these questions about the group or church where you participate regularly.

Note: These items are scored differently from the first four soil sample scales.

Q1: In the last year, how much teaching has your group had on intentionally loving enemies?

Frequently=0 Occasionally=1 Rarely=2 Never=3   Answer _____

Q2: In the last year, how often has your group intentionally attached to people who are upset with you?

Frequently=0 Occasionally=1 Rarely=2 Never=3   Answer _____

Q3: How much "safety to be weak" is there for leaders and members?

High=0 Medium=1 Low=2 None=3   Answer _____

Q4: How much optimism does your group have about discussing topics that might upset someone (particularly someone with influence)?

High=0 Medium=1 Low=2 None=3   Answer ____

Q5: How often are people who justify themselves corrected by the group?

Frequently=0 Occasionally=1 Rarely=2 Never=3   Answer ____

                    Add your answers for a total _____

Scoring your soil sample scale

Add the scores for the five questions. (Your total should be between 0 and 15)

If your total was 0 to 5 your scale score = 1 (Low narcissism)

If your total was 6 to 10 your scale score = 2 (Medium narcissism)

If your total was 11 to 15 your scale score = 3 (High narcissism)

TOTAL SOIL HEALTH SCORE

Confidence

Q1: How long have you been participating in this group?

Less than a year = 1

One to three years = 2

Three or more years = 3

Q2: How many times per week do you usually participate in this group?

Less than once per week = 1

Once per week = 2

More than once per week = 3

Q3: How many times per week does your group usually interact?

Less than once per week = 1

Once per week = 2

More than once per week = 3

Soil Health

S1: Relational Joy score	_____	(Range 1–3)
S2: *Hesed* score	_____	(Range 1–3)
S3: Group Identity score	_____	(Range 1–3)
S4: Correction score	_____	(Range 1–3)
Subtotal	_____	(Range 4–12)
	Minus	
S5: Narcissism score	_____	(Range 1–3)
Total Soil Health	_____	(Range 1–11)

Interpreting your total soil health score:

Total score from 1 to 4 = Failing church

Total score from 5 to 8 = Almost sustainable church

Total score from 9 to 11 = Healthy soil

Appendix B

- - - - - - - - - -

Joy on Demand Exercise

OUR BRAIN NEEDS fuel to run properly. The fuel that our brains were intended to run on is joy. Very simply, joy is what you experience when you can see in another person's face and eyes that they are happy to be with you. God describes this joy in Numbers 6:25: "The LORD make his face shine upon you." God commands the priests to bless people with this phrase. It is also the neurological definition of joy as presented by Dr. Allan Schore, a professor at UCLA. He is known as the Einstein of psychiatry, and as far as we know, he is not a Christian. But he discovered what God already knows: joy is the fuel on which the brain was designed to run.

Our brains have a default emotional state—the state it resides in when other emotions are not temporarily overwhelming it. In the first eighteen months of life, the default emotional state in our brains, which should be joy, is set to one of the six unpleasant emotions that the brain recognizes—sadness, fear, anger, shame, disgust, and hopeless despair. This was not a choice you made. It was set according to what was happening in your life during your infancy.

Here is the good news: we can reset our default emotional state to joy. This happens in our brains as a response to repeated exposure to a state of gratitude. Gratitude is the on-ramp for raising joy in our lives. The Thirty-Day Joy Exercise is a spiritual discipline that will benefit every Christian. Here is how it works:

Gratitude Memories

Think of a memory in your life for which you are grateful. It can be big (the birth of a child) or small (a beautiful sunset). It doesn't matter, as long as you feel gratitude when you think about it.

- Give it a two- to three-word title (for example, "Dan and Dave," "Shining Goldfinch," "Balloon Soccer")
- In a quiet place, go back into this memory and relive it for a minute, like you are back in it
- Ask:
  + What did you feel in your body? Maybe "peace" or "lightness" (it doesn't matter what you feel as long as you feel something in your body)
  + What might God be communicating to you through the memory and the peace you feel? God is with me and likes to share His beauty with me.

Phase 1: Gratitude for Five Minutes

1. Start compiling a list of grateful memories as described above. Each memory has two characteristics: 1) you feel gratitude in your body, and 2) you feel a connection with God in the memory. Eventually, you want a list of at least ten grateful memories.

2. Once a day, spend five minutes residing in gratitude using your list of grateful memories. It is mostly nonverbal. You are feeling a connection with God in your body as you relive memories of gratitude.

Note: Spending five minutes reliving memories without being distracted is difficult if you have never done it before. It will take you a while to be able to sustain the full five minutes without daydreaming or going off on tangents. Give yourself grace. You may be exercising a muscle in your heart that hasn't been used much. Use your list of memories during the five minutes. Some days a single memory will sustain you for five minutes. More commonly, you will need three to five memories to fill five minutes. When the gratitude of one memory starts to fade, go to another one on the list.

Once you can consistently sustain a solid five-minute state of gratitude, you are ready to start the Thirty-Day Joy Exercise.

Phase 2: The Thirty-day Joy Exercise

1. Spend five minutes of gratitude three times a day. Do it the first thing in the morning, at midday, and the last thing you do at night before going to bed. Do this for thirty days. Consistency is key.

2. Sometime during the thirty days, your brain will respond to this repeated exposure to gratitude. It will reset your default emotional state to joy. You will likely start to feel different when you wake up, and you will notice when you slip out of joy as you live your life. *Not feeling joy will feel abnormal to you.* You will want to return to joy as soon as possible.

Phase 3: Joy Maintenance

Maintain joy levels by spending five minutes each day in gratitude.

Appendix C

Pseudo-Joy Checklist

From E. James Wilder, Edward M. Khouri, Chris M. Coursey, Shelia D. Sutton, *Joy Starts Here: The Transformation Zone* (East Peoria, IL: Shepherd's House Inc., 2013). Used by permission.

- I often try to keep my mistakes a secret
- Our diet is too high in comfort foods
- I often keep doing things in secret that make me feel ashamed
- We spend/shop too much
- I can't let go of a past relationship
- I think that someone at home is trying to keep certain behaviors secret
- This past week, I craved things that are not good for me
- I think that someone at home has binges or abuses power
- Relationships feel very confusing to me
- I am close to many people who abuse prescriptions, drugs, or alcohol

Appendix D

- - - - - - - - -

Enemy Mode Checklist

Simple Enemy Mode
(Relational Circuits Off)

- I just want to make a problem, person, or feeling go away
- I don't want to listen to what others feel or say
- My mind is "locked onto" something upsetting
- I don't want to be connected to _____ (someone I usually like)
- I just want to get away, or fight, or I freeze
- I more aggressively interrogate, judge, and fix others

Predatory Enemy Mode
(Relational Circuits without Attachment)

- I am looking, listening, or thinking of any weaknesses I can find in others
- I would like them to lose
- I am plotting my escape or covering my moves

THE OTHER HALF OF CHURCH

- I find my attitude easy to justify that I am right
- Tracking their feelings, movements, and plans feels strategic
- I know what will bother them and how I can use that to my advantage

Compassionate Relational Mode (Relational Circuits Fully On)

- Feel curious (want to know) about what the other is experiencing right now
- I desire to share what the other person is feeling at this moment
- I feel protective of them
- The other person feels like one of my people
- Relationships feel more important than the problem
- I feel aware of God's presence

Appendix E

- - - - - - - - -

Maturity Stages

From E. James Wilder, Edward M. Khouri, Chris M. Coursey, Shelia D. Sutton, *Joy Starts Here: The Transformation Zone* (East Peoria, IL: Shepherd's House Inc., 2013). Used by permission.

THE UNBORN STAGE—Ideal Age: Conception to Birth

While acknowledging that this stage is crucial to the formation of bonds and a working body along with many learned patterns for voices, cries, food preferences, immune system functions, and even a liberal transfer of DNA from the infant into the mother's body to provide stem cells, repair areas of damage in the mother's body, spend the rest of her life in her brain, and other profound life-sharing changes, we will not include any list of tasks and needs for the development of the unborn child in this list.

THE INFANT STAGE—Ideal Age: Birth to Age 4

Infant Needs

- Joy bonds with both parents that are strong, loving, caring, secure
- Important needs are met without asking
- Quiet together time
- Help regulating distressing emotions

- Be seen through the "eyes of heaven"
- Receive and give life
- Have others synchronize with him/her first

Infant Tasks

- Receive with joy
- Learn to synchronize with others
- Organize self into a person through imitation
- Learn to regulate emotions
- Learn to return to joy from every emotion
- Learn to be the same person over time
- Learn self-care skills
- Learn to rest

THE CHILD STAGE—Ideal Age: Ages 4 to 13

Child Needs

- Weaning
- Help to do what he does not feel like doing
- Help sorting feelings, imaginations, and reality
- Feedback on guesses, attempts, and failures
- Be taught the family history
- Be taught the history of God's family
- Be taught the "big picture" of life
- Be taught to do "worthy work" for mind and body

Child Tasks

- Take care of self (one is enough right now)
- Learn to ask for what he/she needs
- Learn self-expression
- Develop personal resources and talents
- Learn to make himself/herself understandable to others
- Learn to do hard things

- Learn what satisfies
- Tame the nucleus accumbens (our cravings)
- See self through the "eyes of heaven"

THE ADULT STAGE—Ideal Age: Age 13 to first child
Adult Needs

- A rite of passage
- Time to bond with peers and form a group identity
- Inclusion by members of the same sex
- Observing the same sex using their power fairly
- Being given important tasks by his/her community
- Guidance for the personal imprint they will make on history
- Opportunities to share life in partnership

Adult Tasks

- Take care of two or more people at the same time
- Discover the main characteristics of his/her heart
- Proclaim and defend personal and community (group) identity
- Bring self and others back to joy simultaneously
- Develop a personal style that reflects his/her heart
- Learn to protect others from himself/herself
- Learn to diversify and blend roles
- Life-giving sexuality
- Mutual satisfaction in a relationship
- Partnership
- To see others through the "eyes of heaven"

THE PARENT STAGE—Ideal Age: From first child until youngest child becomes an adult at 13

Parent Needs

- To give life
- An encouraging partner
- Guidance from elders
- Peer review from other fathers or mothers
- A secure and orderly environment

  - Parent Tasks
  - Giving without needing to receive in return
  - Building a home
  - Protecting his/her family
  - Serving his/her family
  - Enjoying his/her family
  - Helping his/her children reach maturity
  - Synchronizing with the needs of children, spouse, family, work, and church
  - See his/her own children through the "eyes of heaven"

THE ELDER STAGE—Ideal Age: Youngest child is an adult

Elder Needs

- A community to call his/her own
- Recognition by his/her community
- A proper place in the community structure
- Have others trust them
- Be valued and protected by their community

Elder Tasks

- Hospitality
- Giving life to those without families
- Parent and mature his/her community

- Build and maintain a community identity
- Act like himself/herself in the midst of difficulty
- Enjoy what God puts in each person in the community (seeing each of them through "eyes of heaven")
- Building trust of others through the elder's own transparency and spontaneity

NOTE: Each stage builds on the previous stage. Therefore each stage includes the needs and tasks of the previous stage. The "ideal age" is the earliest age at which new tasks can be attempted. The end of that stage expects some degree of mastery. In no way does our maturity determine our value, but it does determine the level of responsibility we can handle.

NOTES

Chapter 1: Half-Brained Christianity

1. Dallas Willard, *Renovation of the Heart: Putting On the Character of Christ* (Colorado Springs, CO: NavPress, 2002).

2. It would be a major mistake to assume that because the control is located in one place in the brain that all the work is being done there. What has been called "left brain" or "right brain" is generally done all over the brain, even when some part of the brain is dominant for the unification of effort. So we will see that joy and identity are right-brain functions. What we mean is that there are tendrils all over the brain that process joy and identity, but the control or unification of all the work is dominantly a right-brain job. There has been a popular misconception about the right and left brain for decades. In this old idea, the right brain is artistic and free while the left brain is rigid and logical. Starting in the 1990s—the decade of the brain—scientists could finally scan living brains burning sugar or oxygen. What followed these studies was another series of mistakes based on the presumption that whatever was burning the most energy was in charge. It was equally possible that what was burning energy was the part that was in trouble.

   The brain is incredibly economical in its use of energy and prefers to use as little energy as possible when things are going as desired and predicted. Studies that focused on high-brain activity, therefore, were subject to a potentially large flaw in their conclusions. They could tell where the "action" was happening but might incorrectly conclude that the action was where a process was controlled as compared to the place where the problems with the process were being resolved. In addition, when activity was high enough, the brain was not doing anything useful at all. At times the brain approached the levels of activity that would be called a "cramp" if it were a muscle. We know that a totally cramped muscle is doing no good for our motion or actions.

   One popular error was concluding that an active left prefrontal cortex with a quiet right prefrontal was "happy," while if the right prefrontal was active instead, the brain was "unhappy." The solution, therefore, was to suppress the right and activate the left so people might have a better mood. It so happened that whenever this change occurred naturally, the person's mood brightened considerably. But suppressing the right and pushing activity in the left did not produce this same improvement. Not until a better explanation was found through the brain science of Dr. Allan Schore and Dr. Antonio Damasio could this be explained.

3. Dallas Willard, "Spiritual Formation as a Natural Part of Salvation," in *Life in the Spirit: Spiritual Formation in Theological Perspective*, ed. Jeffrey P. Greenman and George Kalantzis (Downers Grove, IL: IVP Academic, 2010), 55.

4. A better model of the brain suggests that the part of the brain that is in control (dominant) is relatively quiet when all is well. The faster-than-conscious thought track in the right prefrontal area is dominant for our identity, character, values, and relationships. When all is well in our identity and relationships our right prefrontal areas sits quietly by and lets the slower system, left prefrontal, handle conscious interactions with the world. We are in a happy mood, for all is well with the now quiet relational right brain. When something goes wrong with our identity and significant relationships, the right brain fires up to deal with this distressing problem. The left brain goes into a sort of "standby" level, and we are in distress. The solution is not to shut down the relational repair system so we feel fine. The solution is to find a relational solution to what has taken away our joy. Then the master system will go back to watching the left brain play happily in its conscious speed world.

It would be a second and major mistake to assume that because the control is located one place in the brain that there is where all the work is being done. What has been called "left brain" or "right brain" is generally done all over the brain even when some part of the brain is dominant for the unification of effort.

If we were scanning an airport for where the oxygen was being burned, we would have a difficult time finding the air traffic controllers, the pilots, and the flight management teams. Work would be going on all over the airport, but the control network would not be where most of the work was done. Indeed, we would probably conclude that airports are controlled by coffee nuclei located around the terminals and planes. Activity from these coffee nuclei seems to initiate most airport activities. Sellers of caramel macchiato and soy latte supplements would proclaim that their improved airport operation had prevented flight cancellations.

Until about age four, the two halves of the brain operate in near total disconnection from each other. The two sides have very clearly separate growth times, and what develops as it grows differs very widely. Indeed, much of what goes on in the brain is not open to conscious examination or control. The brain controls our blood pressure, for example. If we could watch and control blood pressure, we would certainly "turn it down" rather than have a stroke, but this is not to be. The effect of not being able to observe many processes has been to try to do too much with the processes we can observe. This error has encroached on Christianity as we have reduced identity, knowledge, and truth to only what we can consciously observe. To understand what we say about the left and right brain, including how we learn to be both human and Christian, we must move beyond these old understandings.

5. See Paul Helm, *Human Nature from Calvin to Edwards* (Grand Rapids, MI: Reformation Heritage Books, 2018), 239. N. T. Wright, "Loving to

Know," *First Things*, February 2020, https://www.firstthings.com /article/2020/02/loving-to-know, retrieved 02/27/2020.

6. Antonio Damasio, *Descartes' Error: Emotion, Reason, and the Human Brain* (New York: Avon Books, 1994), 245–252.

7. Helm, *Human Nature*, 34–35.

Chapter 2: How Do People Grow?

1. Dallas Willard, *Renovation of the Heart: Putting On the Character of Christ* (Colorado Springs, CO: NavPress, 2002), 238.

2. Michel Hendricks, *Basic Training for Walking with Jesus* (self-pub., CreateSpace, 2018).

3. Willard, *Renovation of the Heart*, 243.

4. Dallas Willard, *The Divine Conspiracy: Rediscovering Our Hidden Life in God* (New York: HarperCollins Publishers, 1998), 301.

5. Dallas Willard, *The Great Omission: Rediscovering Jesus' Essential Teachings on Discipleship* (New York: HarperCollins Publishers, 2006).

6. Willard, *Renovation of the Heart*, 239.

7. Dallas Willard, *The Spirit of the Disciplines: Understanding How God Changes Lives* (San Francisco: HarperOne, 1999), 235.

8. Ibid., 16.

9. Willard, *Renovation of the Heart*, 112.

10. E. James Wilder, Edward M. Khouri, Chris M. Coursey, Shelia D. Sutton, *Joy Starts Here: The Transformation Zone* (East Peoria, IL: Shepherd's House Inc., 2013), 87.

11. James K. A. Smith, *You Are What You Love: The Spiritual Power of Habit* (Grand Rapids, MI: Brazos Press, 2016), 3.

12. Paul Helm, *Human Nature from Calvin to Edwards* (Grand Rapids, MI: Reformation Heritage Books, 2018) treats this at length. Also see Nathan O. Hatch and Harry S. Stout, eds., *Jonathan Edwards and the American Experience* (New York: Oxford University Press, 1988).

13. Marcus Warner and E. James Wilder, *The Solution of Choice: Four Good Ideas that Neutralized Western Christianity* (Carmel, IN: Deeper Walk International, 2018), 29–34.

14. Willard, *Renovation of the Heart*, 243

15. Allen C. Guelzo, *Edwards on the Will: A Century of American Theological Debate* (Middletown, CT: Wesleyan University Press, 1989).

16. *The Solution of Choice* explains this more fully. Also Smith writes about this in *You Are What You Love*.

17. You can find more information about Thrive training at thrivetoday.org/ thrive/.

Chapter 3: Joy: The Face of Jesus That Transforms

1. Cyd Holsclaw and Geoff Holsclaw, *Does God Really Like Me?: Discovering the God Who Wants to Be with Us* (Downers Grove, IL: IVP Books, 2020), 83. The authors write about God's joy to be with us.

2. Daniel J. Siegel and Mary Hartzell, *Parenting from the Inside Out: How a Deeper Self-Understanding Can Help You Raise Children Who Thrive* (New York: Penguin, 2014), 38.

3. Jesus sings Psalm 22 while on the cross, "My God, My God, why have you forsaken me?" This has often been preached as "the Father turned His face away," but this statement is not in Scripture.
4. Holsclaw and Holsclaw, *Does God Really Like Me?*, 43.
5. E. James Wilder, Edward M. Khouri, Chris M. Coursey, Shelia D. Sutton, *Joy Starts Here: The Transformation Zone* (East Peoria, IL: Shepherd's House Inc., 2013), 35.
6. E. James Wilder, Anna Kang, John Loppnow, and Sungshim Loppnow, *Joyful Journey: Listening to Immanuel* (East Peoria, IL: Shepherd's House Inc., 2015), 16.
7. For information on this training, go to www.thrivetoday.org/thrive/.
8. For more information on this training and more, see ThriveToday.org.
9. Wilder et al., *Joy Starts Here*, 205–206.
10. Marcus Warner and Chris Coursey, *The 4 Habits of Joy-Filled Marriages: How 15 Minutes a Day Will Help You Stay in Love* (Chicago: Moody Publishers, 2019).
11. Track 1 of Thrive training explains this cycle thoroughly and gives you many chances to practice it. See thrivetoday.org/thrive for more information.

Chapter 4: *Hesed*: Our Relational Glue

1. Jim and Marcus have devoted a chapter to this topic in Marcus Warner and E. James Wilder, *The Solution of Choice: Four Good Ideas That Neutralized Western Christianity* (Carmel, IN: Deeper Walk International, 2018), 67–79.
2. Jim Wilder, *Renovated: God, Dallas Willard and the Church that Transforms* (Colorado Springs, CO: NavPress, 2020), 107–128, 201–208. Jim has written about *agape* in his dialogue with Dallas Willard in *Renovated*. *Renovated* includes discussion of the Hebrew and Greek words for "glue" and the commands to glue ourselves to God. This is the same meaning as the psychological word "bond." In addition, *Renovated* reviews the twelve characteristics of a strong and healthy attachment, comparing them with scriptural instructions for life with God and others. The twelve characteristics of a good bond match strongly with a biblical way of life.
3. Attachment outpowers sexuality and grows through joy. However, when joy fades and people are no longer glad to be together, new joys can grow new attachments where they should not grow. Thus, we find well-known leaders and powerful people becoming attached to the wrong people in spite of knowing all there is to know about how they should live. When attachment and sex drives combine, there is no force left in the human mind that can fight them. When we realize that our attachments grow through joy, it becomes clear that we should be diligent about keeping joy high where joy is meant to be grown.
4. E. James Wilder, *The Pandora Problem: Facing Narcissism in Leaders and Ourselves* (Carmel, IN: Deeper Walk International, 2018), 20–27.
5. E. James Wilder, *The Complete Guide to Living with Men* (Pasadena, CA: Shepherd's House Inc., 2004), 16.
6. Wilder, *The Complete Guide*, 16.

7. James G. Friessen, E. James Wilder, Anne M. Bierling, Rick Koepcke, and Maribeth Poole, *Living from the Heart Jesus Gave You* (East Peoria, IL: Shepherd's House, Inc., 2013), 58–69.
8. In *You Are What You Love: The Spiritual Power of Habit* (Grand Rapids, MI: Brazos Press, 2016), James K. A. Smith argues that we have made people to be brains on a stick as a result of Enlightenment thinking.
9. Warner and Wilder, *Solution of Choice*, 67.
10. Ibid., 68.
11. Robert H. Mounce, *The Book of Revelation,* The New International Commentary on the New Testament (Grand Rapids, MI: Eerdmans Publishing Company, 1977), 88–89.
12. C. S. Lewis, *The Four Loves* (New York: HarperCollins Publishers, 1960), Kindle Edition, 154.
13. E. James Wilder, Edward M. Khouri, Chris M. Coursey, Shelia D. Sutton, *Joy Starts Here: The Transformation Zone* (East Peoria, IL: Shepherd's House Inc., 2013), 112.

Chapter 6: Healthy Correction: Stop Being So Nice

1. Curt Thompson, *The Soul of Shame: Retelling the Stories We Believe about Ourselves* (Downers Grove, IL: IVP Books, 2015), ch. 3, "Joy, Shame and the Brain."
2. We have mentioned all seven. Six are big emotions wired into the brain. The seventh is the attachment pain mentioned in the chapter on *hesed*.
3. E. James Wilder, *The Pandora Problem: Facing Narcissism in Leaders and Ourselves* (Carmel, IN: Deeper Walk International, 2018), 151–60.
4. Wilder, *The Pandora Problem*, 155.
5. *The Pandora Problem* has exercises on healthy shame messages at the end of each chapter. *The Pandora Problem Companion Guide* also provides opportunities to practice this skill.
6. Wilder, *The Pandora Problem*, 111.

Chapter 7: Narcissism: The Relational Infection

1. E. James Wilder, *The Pandora Problem: Facing Narcissism in Leaders and Ourselves* (Carmel, IN: Deeper Walk International, 2018), 155.
2. Wilder, *The Pandora Problem*, 45–46.
3. Ibid., 12–18.
4. Definitions of narcissism differ in America and Europe among professionals, and the line at which narcissism becomes a psychological disorder is not firmly established. The diagnostic category of narcissistic personality disorder has been dissolved in favor of making narcissism a more general personality difficulty.
5. Wilder, *The Pandora Problem*, 131–50.
6. See *Joyful Journey* in the Resources at the end of this chapter for more information.
7. *The Pandora Problem Companion Guide* contains these exercises.
8. Wilder, *The Pandora Problem*, 235–55.

Chapter 8: A Full-Brained Christianity

1. For example, Acts 24:3 and 26:2.
2. The training is based on the Life Model created by Jim Wilder. My wife and I are specifically going through Thrive, a full-brained relational skills training based on the Life Model. See thrivetoday.org/thrive.
3. You can read more about maturity levels in *Living from the Heart Jesus Gave You* and *Complete Guide to Living with Men*.
4. For more information, read *Joyful Journey* by Wilder et al. and the extensive writings and videos of Karl D. Lehman MD at KCLehman.com.
5. Dallas Willard, *Hearing God: Developing a Conversational Relationship with God* (Downers Grove, IL: InterVarsity Press, 1984).
6. Wilder, *The Pandora Problem*, 190.
7. We know how natural families can come to control church environments and become a pastor's worst nightmare. We are describing relationships like Paul and Timothy, Paul and Titus, that would qualify as discipleship.
8. Read chapter 2 of *Living from the Heart Jesus Gave You* for more information on maturity. Thrive Training is designed to fill in all missing infant level relational skills. See thrivetoday.org/thrive.
9. For more maturity signs, see *Living from the Heart Jesus Gave You*, 53–57.

REVIVE YOUR LEADERSHIP.
GROW HEALTHY TEAMS.
SEE GREAT RESULTS.

HOW TO MAKE DISCIPLES
USING HOSPITALITY

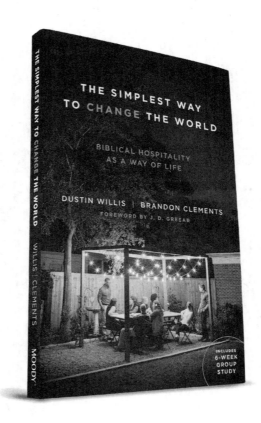

MOODY Publishers®

From the Word to Life®

The Simplest Way to Change the World guides readers in the lost art of Christian hospitality. Author Dustin Willis offers principles and practices for adopting hospitality as a lifestyle, shows how it is one of today's most effective missions models, and explores its challenges and many benefits.

978-0-8024-1497-7 | also available as eBook and audiobook

"Few books have the potential to change your life as much as this one."

—Lee Strobel

Your Future Self Will Thank You is a compassionate and humorous guide to reclaiming your willpower. It shares proven, practical strategies for success, as well as biblical principles that will help you whether you want to lose a few pounds, conquer addiction, or kick your nail-biting habit.

978-0-8024-1829-6 | also available as eBook and audiobook

DOES YOUR LIFE EVER FEEL LIKE ONE SERIES OF RUSHED MOMENTS AFTER ANOTHER?